$12\frac{52}{}$

BLACK FILM AS GENRE

Way Down South, RKO

BLACK FILM AS GENRE

Thomas Cripps

Indiana University Press • Bloomington and London

Library of Congress Cataloging in Publication Data

Cripps, Thomas.
   Black film as genre.
   Bibliography: p.
   Filmography: p.
   Includes index.
   1. Afro-Americans in motion pictures. I. Title.
PN1995.9.N4C68   791.43'0909'352   77–23630
ISBN 0–253–37502–9   1 2 3 4 5 82 81 80 79 78

Contents

For my mother and my sister

Preface

"Genre film is a trick we play on the dead," Voltaire might have said had he returned to life and been appointed to a chair in popular culture at Nanterre, and he would have had a point. Yet, actually, it is the historian or critic who plays the trick by fabricating a systematic means of examining the film.

Nevertheless, the filmmaker and the audience have silently conspired to create pleasing, informative, and evocative formulas, atmospheres, symbols, and themes that make up the recipe for popular genre films. In turn, the historian and critic incur a debt to sensitive and talkative audiences in the form of successive generations of students who respond to the genre. For their insights in class, in conversation, in papers, and in research projects, I owe a special debt to my students at Morgan State University and Stanford (in 1969–1970): Sidney Cousin, Pat Feaster, Everett Marshburn, A. Ricardo Perry, Preston Winkler, Robert Bunn, Clarence Davis, Pamela Jones, and Michael Fuller.

I am grateful for insights shared in conversations with Lucia Lynn Moses, Harry Popkin, Ben Rinaldo, Jim Hoberman, Ken Jacobs, William Greaves, Ernie Smith, Carlton Moss, Stuart Heisler, Frank Capra, Erik Barnouw, David Culbert, Horace Coleman, Melvin Van Peebles, Ronald Goldwyn, Clayton Riley, Pearl Bowser, Ted Toddy, Michael Roemer, and Lester Sack. I have been permitted almost unlimited opportunities to study the generic films that make up the body of this book through the good offices and generosity of many persons. My greatest debts I owe to the unfailing kindness of the staff of the Library of Congress Motion Picture Section, William T. Murphy of the Audio-Visual Section of the Archives of the United States, Frank Holland of the National Film Library in Aston Clinton, Helen Cyr and her staff of the Audio-Visual Department of the Enoch Pratt Free Library, Professor Robert Carringer and the Film Collection of the University of Illinois, Nate Zelikow, and John Baker.

A considerable burden of moonlit editorial work was done while I was working on another project during a year in Washington as a Rockefeller Humanities Fellow and a resident Fellow of the Woodrow Wilson International Center for Scholars. I am grateful to the Rockefeller Foundation and to the Woodrow Wilson Center, and its director, James Billington, and his staff, for their generous support. The Woodrow Wilson Fellows provided scholarly comradeship that inspired my work. Ann Bain, Sue Gnagy, and Doug Kelso made the index, for which I am in their debt.

Finally, I owe thanks to Barbara Humphrys of the Library of Congress, Everett Marshburn of the Maryland Center for Public Broadcasting, Professor J.R. Lyston of Essex Community College, and Professor Michael Bayton of Morgan State University, for their careful reading and criticism of the manuscript. My wife, Alma Taliaferro Cripps, and my children, Ben, Alma, and Paul, all contributed to the stimulating life out of which this book emerged.

Black Film as Genre

PART ONE

1 Definitions

The agenda is set by the formula.
—Erik Barnouw, in conversation.

For the purposes of this study, "black film" may be defined as those motion pictures made for theater distribution that have a black producer, director, and writer, or black performers; that speak to black audiences or, incidentally, to white audiences possessed of preternatural curiosity, attentiveness, or sensibility toward racial matters; and that emerge from self-conscious intentions, whether artistic or political, to illuminate the Afro-American experience. In the latter part of this century, this definition might be expanded to include major motion pictures and other projects made for television, as well as films that, despite foreign origins in, say, Africa, speak to Afro-American concerns.

If we were to bring this definition to a fine pinpoint, we should argue forever over who has the right to dance on the head of the pin. The Lincoln Motion Picture Company, founded in 1916, always used a white cameraman; Oscar Micheaux, especially after depression-induced bankruptcy, accepted "white" financing; *Variety* frequently evaluated so-called race movies, thereby possibly influencing their makers. Thus almost every black film, from production through distribution, was affected by whites.

Black film taken in its narrowest sense then consists of only a tiny body of work seen by a coterie of black moviegoers, then consigned to an early death in dusty storerooms, not to be seen again until brought to light in "white" repositories like the Library of Congress.

By this standard the best single example of black film seen as pure product—produced by blacks, for blacks, and with an ambition to advance the image or the cause of the race—is the fragmented evangelistic film of Eloise Gist, the traveling black preacher. She ranged over the South during the Great Depression, spreading her revivalist faith through motion pictures shot only for the specific narrow purpose defined by her own faith and spirit. Nowhere from script to screen did any white hand intrude, or any white eye observe. Neither white financing in the beginning nor white appreciation at the end affected her pristine black fundamentalism. Her films were naive, technically primitive, literal depictions of black Southern religious folklore that brought faith to life, much as an illuminated manuscript gave visual life to Christian lore in the Middle Ages.

But the entire body of such black film could be seen in a single day's session at a Steenbeck viewer. Our definition of black film must necessarily be broader so as to include the work of those self-conscious black artists who were at least as interested in the beauty of the medium as in the effectiveness of the message; the black filmmaker whose work emerged from the conventional channels of production that were lined with white money, advice, and control, even down to "final cut" approval; and finally, though rarely, film produced by white filmmakers whose work attracted the attention, if not always the unconditional praise, of black moviegoers and critics.

A broader compass also allows us to avoid the trap of claiming too much black control of certain films. In recent years many critics, inspired by the heady atmosphere of pursuit and discovery of old and presumably lost black film, have made exaggerated, unwarranted claims of certain instances of monolithic black control of the filmmaking process.

In the late 1920s, for example, the Colored Players Company of Philadelphia turned out a reputedly good film version of a famous black novel; a curiously tragic black revival of the old temperance tract, *Ten Nights in a Bar Room* (1926), starring the eminent black actor, Charles Gilpin, in his only screen appearance; and, most significant, *The Scar of Shame* (1927), an evocative, sometimes delicate drama of color caste distinctions within Afro-American circles. The recent discovery of this last film resulted in a round of showings to both black and white students, and a rash of essays saluting its presumably black originators, the creative force who looked over the shoulders of the obviously Italian technicians cited in the credits. And yet, a few moments of cursory research revealed that from top to bottom, the Colored Players were actually white, save for their front man, Sherman "Uncle Dud" Dudley, an old black vaudevillian who had dreams of a black Hollywood on the outskirts of Washington.

Perhaps because of the hazards inherent in drawing fine distinctions, black critics have avoided the task of constructing a black cinema aesthetic, at least until recently. Addison Gayle's otherwise admirable *The Black Aesthetic* (1971), for example, does not include a single sample of cinema comment. The little criticism that appears often splinters into two camps differing in focus: the one literary, the other political. The opposing sides in this argument either demand that art be a weapon against racism, or feel that art is neither bullet nor ballot. In any case, the debate has done little to help define the outlines of a black aesthetic or of black genre film.

At the center of this controversy is the "twoness" of American racial life. The term was coined by W.E.B. DuBois, the premier black intellectual of the twentieth century. It describes the anomaly of American racial arrangements, which segregate black from white, discriminate along racial lines, and yet oblige Afro-Americans to assimilate the values of white America. If films reflect the belief and behavior systems of society, we must expect that they will express these realities.

Thus, given the persistence of American racial codes, it does not seem possible, except in a unique case like Eloise Gist's film, that either a black or white filmmaker could produce a film that in some way did not suffer alteration of tone, plot, theme, pace, or character,

1. Harold Garrison (center), King Vidor's black assistant director on *Hallelujah!,* on location near Memphis. With several native black Southerners, he helped provide an authentic ambience. (Wanda Tuchock Collection)

and even benefitted from, the occasional interracial collaboration. For example, the presumably black *The Scar of Shame* was produced by a film crew that was largely white. Two years later, in 1929, King Vidor's MGM opus, *Hallelujah!,* an appreciative styling of black rural folk religion, profited from the advice of Harold Garrison, a black crew member, as well as from a panel of black Southern preachers, who gave counsel while the company shot on location along the Mississippi. The veteran black actor, Clarence Muse, performed a similar function on the set of Fox's *Hearts in Dixie* (1929) and in other Hollywood films, one of which he and Langston Hughes wrote for Sol Lesser.

But it was in the area of financing where blacks and whites really came together, even outside the realm of Hollywood. Even the most independent producers of race movies—those films made for exclusively black audiences between 1916 and 1956—relied on white sources of capital, distributors, bookers, and exhibitors. Life on the movie set was not significantly different from American life at large. Whites bossed and blacks labored, with only a little bargaining room between them.

After the film was in the can, blacks and whites still shared power over the fate of the product. From the earliest days of filmmaking at the beginning of the century, censors' scissors shaped film imagery and themes. But the Negro minister who sat on Chicago's board of censors was a rarity, so over the years, blacks tended to accommodate the wishes of white censors. In 1924 a black independent filmmaker, Oscar Micheaux, reshaped his *Body and Soul* to suit the New York state film censor. As late as 1970, Melvin Van Peebles, the most celebrated of recent black filmmakers, was outraged by the censorious and delimiting "X" rating given his *Sweet Sweetback's Baadasssss Song* by the white Motion Picture Association of America, a stigma that denied him access to a prospective black adolescent audience. Also by the 1970s, much documentary film was conditioned by its sponsorship and support by the public television network, with its charter obligation to reach all segments of the national audience. Moreover, "white" film sometimes took on a black hue as a result of favorable black responses, such as Congressman Oscar DePriest's endorsement of *Hallelujah!* in 1929 and James P. Murray's praise of Michael Roemer's *Nothing But a Man* (1964) in *Black Creation,* a magazine of Afro-American arts.

A glance at American racial history reinforces this broadened view of black cinema. In the past black creativity has been at its most clearly "black" in those endeavors *into which* blacks were most segregated from white influence—work songs, gospel songs, spirituals, and theological rhetoric. Even in these accomplishments, however, an occasional white European echo may be heard. But if James Agee is correct when he insists that black art is at its most tainted, and even corrupt, when it is exposed to white praise, we must also see that blacks in racially integrated circumstances have been equally creative. Their work, a syncretism of Africa and Europe, is given shape, substance, and meaning by both traditions. Thus blacks in the arts—architecture, symphonic music, nonrepresentational painting, and even fiction—work in European forms and conventions while preserving trace elements of Afro-American culture.

The game of basketball is an illustrative case of differing racial styles of expression within a system of formal rules and conventions. A form of competitive choreography based on rules laid out at a white YMCA college in Massachusetts, the game is leavened by contrasting styles of white and black play, the former deliberate and long-range, the latter, shaped by childhood training in constricted playgrounds, fast-paced and close-range. But both are basketball.

If black intellectuals ever hoped to break from the constraints of American racial segregation, then Hollywood liberalism with its sentimental faith in progress, goodness, and individual worth provided a strong incentive that kept many blacks pressing toward eventual racial integration. Nevertheless, this same racial liberalism held out unrealistic hopes that diverted black filmmakers away from racial independence, sometimes by enabling them to join the major studios, sometimes by imitating Hollywood genres. Particularly after 1920 as Hollywood was becoming a world cinema capital, black screen roles increased in quantity and sometimes quality.

Year after year *Uncle Tom's Cabin* (1927), *Hallelujah!*, *Hearts in Dixie*, *The Green Pastures* (1936), *Slave Ship* (1937), *So Red the Rose* (1935), *Beggars of Life* (1928), *Crash Dive* (1943), *Sahara* (1943), *Bataan* (1943), *Pinky* (1949), *Stormy Weather* (1943), *Cabin in the Sky* (1943), *Raisin in the Sun* (1961), *Lilies of the Field* (1963), *The Defiant Ones* (1958), and *Sounder* (1972) promised an ever hopeful future. Much like a happy ending, progress at least seemed possible on the screen if not in real life. Unfortunately, few pictures left Afro-Americans with a completely satisfying portrait of American life, for even so-called problem pictures and message movies of the 1940s did not offer an agenda for eventual social change. Nevertheless, as the films reinforced hope, they diverted black attention away from the goal of an independent black cinema.

It is this dual aspect of movies that forces us to view film through some critical prism that takes into account the interracial teamwork that goes into filmmaking. The team is rarely all black, and even when blacks predominate, they often come from different economic or regional backgrounds. Black film must be seen as a genre, then, for what it says and how it is said, rather than who is saying it.

Like the French semiological critics who borrow from the science of structural linguistics, we shall seek to define black genre film through social and anthropological rather than aesthetic factors. In this light, films are different from those fine arts in which the artist and his audience share a fund of common knowledge and experience. Rather, films bridge the gap between producer and mass audience, not through shared arcane tastes, but because a team of filmmakers shares a knowledge of genre formulas, more than an artistic tradition, with its audience.

Furthermore, genre films, like folktales and tribal lore, may transmit social meanings beyond the conscious intention of the filmmaker, as well as meaning brought by the audience's own social and cultural history. Moreover, the likelihood of attracting a mass audience is further assured because such films emerged from a history that followed "the novel's way" of telling popular and easily followed stories.

In this popular sense, a shot is a sentence in a tale, as well as a value-laden poetic image. The shot-as-visual-sentence is at the heart of genre film. Shots, like sentences and unlike words, are infinite in number, and therefore unlimited in what they convey and how they are perceived by the audience. The filmmaker composes the shot, constructs the space and the figures in it (and their size), and manipulates these elements as symbols for an audience whose own cultural conditioning limits and directs perceptions.

Thus filmmakers and audiences share a few intensely powerful symbols set in an easily followed narrative form that defines the genre. In many gangster films, the action necessarily opens on wet streets and darkened alleys with the hero, muffled in a trenchcoat, alone in the shadows, set apart from both cops and crooks, upholding a personal code that neither understands. In skilled hands, such repeated, codified images take on meanings larger than themselves and become powerful icons that need few words to explain them. Indeed, they become unintelligible only when the images are cluttered and the ambience is broken by extraneous materials.

When images are repeated and codified into a formula which is presented as a narrative, the resulting genre film permits instant communication between maker and audience. In the case of black film, the basic formula, by emphasizing one or another of its parts, permits expansion into subgenres that are variations on the basic traits. The viewer may see the black genre exemplified in social drama, cautionary tales, musicals, documentaries, religious tracts, and romances featuring both urbane and pastoral heroes.

Nevertheless, the subgenres share a common fund of integrated caste marks that identify the larger genre. Black genre films emerge from a segregated point of view, even when treating "white" themes, and rely on an appropriate repertoire of symbols. These might include a *folk idiom* such as black religion, an urbane *jive idiom* evolved from the lives of jazzmen, or the aloof mask of behavior that might be called *aesthetique du cool*. These idioms then form the perimeters of black social manners expressed both externally, to whites, and internally. Like so many black experiences that receive too much white attention, these modes may become less genuine as they become the subjects of show business routines, in the same way that some gospel music becomes flashy and secular removed from the church and hyped for the stage. The symbolic content of black genre film is given moral urgency by a *tone of advocacy* rather than, say, a reportorial style. Because genre film conveys shared experiences, some of which may not have touched all of the audience with equal impact, the films may employ the literary device of *anatomy* as a means of understanding the whole of black life through the depiction of its parts. Genre film acts as a *ritual* celebrating a *myth,* that is, a value-impregnated tale that is truer than mere truth. Movies made for black genre audiences may range from black versions of Horatio Alger's success stories to Southern Baptist fundamentalism. Finally, the black genre rests on *heroic figures,* either urban or pastoral, each reflecting a different focus of black experience. The urban hero, for example, corresponds roughly to the romantic white westerner, greater than his adversaries only in degree, never mythically greater in quality. A revenge motive is often at the core of his being. He either struggles against it, redeemed and improved by the experience, or he surrenders to it, thereby avenging the pain of history, but at the price of lost innocence.

Although whites may see every black hero as a picaroon, a separation between urban and rural types is clear. The hero's response to the opportunity for revenge often marks him either as a pastoral or a picaresque hero. Much like the western loner, the pastoral hero stands apart from society, secure in his own identity and values; unlike the white westerner, however, he uses the family as his anchor. He is in Northrop Frye's "low mimetic mode" of heroism, superior to neither milieu nor men. He wins not by prevailing but by enduring. The urban picaresque hero, on the other hand, is alone, moved to vengeance, prone to violence modulated only by Shaft's cool professionalism or Sweetback's hope for eventual revolution. Not since Stepin Fetchit has there been a truly ironic black hero, inferior to both men and milieu, but nevertheless surviving by his wits, like Bre'r Rabbit, the African trickster removed to southern America.

Genre film can easily become exploitation film, through which tastes are teased but no deeper needs are met. While genre film tends to treat things as they are and avoids the trap of advocating them, exploitation film sensationalizes them. Genre film merely speaks from a segregated point of view; exploitation film prefers it. Black genre film ritualizes the myth of winning; exploitation film, at its worst, merely celebrates and dramatizes revenge as though it were a form of winning.

Black genre film celebrates *aesthetique du cool,* the outward detachment, composed choreographic strides, and self-possessed, enigmatic mask over inner urgency that have been admired in both Africa and Afro-America. In contrast, so-called "blaxploitation" film trumps *aesthetique du cool* into mere sneering and bravado. The black genre chooses hyperbole as a mode of celebrating the combination of triumph over adversity, fellow feeling, and moral superiority of the oppressed, known most recently as "soul"; "blaxploitation" film only bleats in shrill imitation. The anatomy of black life in black genre film is an instrument of communication *to* the group *by* the group, exemplified by the black CIA agents in *The Spook Who Sat by the Door* (1973), who share their nostalgia for the details of black college life, fraternal orders, and sports; "blaxploitation" film redundantly depicts only what has been done *to* blacks, not *by* them. Individual anatomical details also establish credibility, for example, when the same agents reminisce about the Penn Relays, a sporting event that only a few blacks would remember as the famed "Negro Olympics" of the 1930s and 1940s. In this sense, black genre film is like the black magazine that runs soul food recipes, or the black student newspaper that features a glossary of black argot—they are treatises for the uninitiated on the uses and beauties derived from cultivating a black identity.

Despite rivalry from exploiters, black genre film has survived for half a century, a most remarkable feat in view of the fact that cultural artifacts of an industrial society are often short-lived. To adapt Bronislaw Malinowski, black genre films have, like good tribal lore, expressed, enhanced, and codified belief; safeguarded and enforced group values; offered practical rules of conduct; and vouched for the efficacy of tribal ritual and gods. No other genre, except perhaps the American western, spoke so directly to the meaning and importance of shared values embraced by its audience.

2   The Evolution of Black Film

From the very beginning of American cinema in the 1890s, Afro-Americans appeared on the screen. One might argue that these early films were not truly black because their function, more or less, was to tell whites about the black curiosa on the periphery of their culture. Early topical vignettes in Thomas Edison's films included watermelon-eating contests, Negroes leading parades, black soldiers in Cuba, reenactments of campaigns against guerrillas in the Philippines, and fragments of anthropological ephemera such as West Indian women dancing, coaling ships, or bathing babies. There were occasional bits, such as Biograph's *A Bucket of Cream Ale* (1904), which was drawn from a vaudeville routine in which a "Dutchman" is hit in the face with a growler of beer tossed by his blackfaced maid. In a small way these films attained a range of black imagery that has gone remarkably unnoticed. In their day, the films were black only in the sense that they thrust a heretofore invisible image upon general American viewers. Their roots emerged from a faddish popular anthropology that had been a fountainhead of European exploration in Africa, complete with rival expeditions in search of the sources of the Nile, voyages to polar icecaps, attempts by the U.S. Department of the Interior to collect Indian lore, and even white-water adventures down the Colorado River. Therefore many early black figures on the screen were no more than the subjects of a quest for the legendary, the curious, and the bizarre, through darkest Africa and Carib isle. Along with stray vaudeville routines and gag shots, occasional faithfully recorded visual records appeared, such as that of Theodore Roosevelt's journey to Africa and *The Military Drill of the Kikuyu Tribes and Other Native Ceremonies* (1914). In another vein, cameramen pursued the black heavyweight champion Jack Johnson, either to record his frequent breaches of racial etiquette or to document his hoped-for eventual defeat.

But if early films, lacking as they were in black sources, point of view, or advocacy, whetted black appetites, they hardly could have satisfied them. In fact, within a dozen years of their beginnings, the early black appearances were snuffed out by a renewed fascination with the Civil War era brought on by the approach of its Golden Anniversary. During these early years, amidst the stereotyped crapshooters, chicken thieves, and coon shows that the screen inherited from Southern popular literature, movies also offered, in addition to reportorial film of exotic locales, Edwin S. Porter's *Uncle Tom's Cabin* (1903) with its wisp of Abolitionism and a flurry of authentic cakewalking. A genuine bit of "rubberlegs" dancing in Biograph's *The Fights of Nations* (1907) was another example of occasional deviations from Southern metaphor. But after 1910 the celebration of the Civil War removed almost all authentic depiction of black Americans from the nation's screens, the semicentennial serving as an inspiration to put aside realism in favor of romantic nostalgia as a mode for presenting Negroes on film.

In a movie world populated by Afro-Americans who embraced slavery, loved the Union but not the principle of Abolition, expressed their deepest humanity through loyal service to white masters, and counted the master class, its families, and fortunes above their own, there could not have been a genuinely black film. The movie slaves either served the white cause in such films as *A Slave's Devotion* (1913), *Old Mammy's Charge* (1914), *The Littlest Rebel* (1914), *His Trust* (1911), *His Trust Fulfilled* (1911), and *Old Mammy's Secret Code* (1913), or they at least stood by passively, lending atmosphere to the Southern setting in *The Empty Sleeve* (1914), *Days of War* (ca. 1914), *For the Cause of the South* (1914), *A Fair*

Rebel (1914), *The Soldier Brothers of Susannah* (1912), and literally hundreds more.

Coincident with these social forces, the editorial techniques of filmmaking had been growing more sophisticated. In 1915, D. W. Griffith, a sentimental Southerner with a feel for Victorian melodrama and a keen visual sense, synthesized nearly a decade's observation and practice into a film of unprecedented three-hour length—*The Birth of a Nation*—and sold it through the grandest publicity campaign ever given a motion picture. The film was an illiberal racial tract that celebrated Southern slavery, the fortitude of the Ku Klux Klan, and the fealty of "good Negroes."

The national Negro leadership, just beginning to enjoy the fruits of a quarter century of experiment (and tinkering with various Afro-American Leagues, the National Negro Business League, the Niagara Movement, and the like), came together in the National Association for the Advancement of Colored People. Its urbane bourgeois members, including many whites, felt singularly offended by the hoary Southern metaphors signified by Griffith's imagery. Unfortunately for the future of black film, they countered with censorship rather than filmmaking, resulting in a briefly successful campaign that unwittingly had the long-range effect of driving all but the most comic black roles from the screen.

During the year following *The Birth of a Nation,* black genre film began in earnest. Although newspaper stories hinted of a few early attempts in the Middle West—notably those of Bill Foster—the first two genuinely black film companies were those organized by Emmett J. Scott and the brothers George and Noble Johnson.

Scott's group promised more, but perhaps because it came first, suffered the more resounding failure. Scott, a former Texas newspaperman and Booker T. Washington's secretary at Tuskegee Institute for almost twenty years, looked to filmmaking as a first step to his independence after the death of the authoritarian Washington in 1915. At first Scott, together with the NAACP, pursued an impossible course, making *Lincoln's Dream,* a film graced with the scholarly

Birth of a Race Photoplay Corporation

For a Million Dollar Picture

To Be Produced in Association With the

SELIG POLYSCOPE COMPANY
William N. Selig, President

ORGANIZED for the production and exhibition of the master photoplay, *THE BIRTH OF A RACE*—an entertaining motion picture of racial understanding. The true story of the Negro—his life in Africa, his transportation to America, his enslavement, his freedom, his achievements, together with his past, present and future relations to his white neighbor and to the world in which both live and labor.

Executive Offices

Birth of a Race Photoplay Corporation

Suite 416, 29 South La Salle Street

Telephone Randolph 2553

CHICAGO, ILLINOIS

2. The cover page of the stock prospectus of the Birth of a Race Corporation demonstrates the desire to develop a black film genre based on race pride as early as 1916. (Julius Rosenwald Papers, The University of Chicago Library)

credentials of historian Albert Bushnell Hart, written by a veteran scriptwriter, financed by matching funds from the NAACP and Universal Pictures, and showcased in a prestigious premiere. Unfortunately, Carl Laemmle of Universal, the prospective "angel," backed off. When the NAACP was paralyzed by a resulting internal debate, Scott was forced to take up negotiations with a small and greedy Chicago firm.

The resulting *Birth of a Race* (1919) suffered from the absence of a strong black voice in defense of a film concept, scattered and often deferred shooting schedules and locations ranging from Chicago to Tampa, and a theme and plot that shifted its emphasis from a biblical to a pacifist idea conditioned by the coming of World War I. After almost three years of shooting and cutting, most of all the black elements had been pushed aside by presumably more timely and universal themes. Despite a glittering opening in Chicago and a few additional bookings, the film dropped from sight and Scott gave up cultivating prospective black middle-class investors in a film project.

Nevertheless, the project attracted the attention of the Johnsons: George, then a postman in Omaha, and Noble, a Universal contract player. In 1916, together with black investors from Los Angeles and a white cameraman, Harry Gant, they had set out to make motion pictures with a black point of view.

Like most of the black middle class in the 1920s, they embraced the American success myth brought to light by Horatio Alger. Between 1916 and 1922, the Johnsons' Lincoln Motion Picture Company averaged almost one film per year, each filled with individualist heroes, who promised blacks the hope of success and the conquest of despair. *By Right of Birth* (1921) was an anatomy of the genteel black upper class of Los Angeles. It starred Clarence Brooks, who later appeared in John Ford's *Arrowsmith* (1931), and Anita Thompson, a tall, stylish actress from the cast of *Runnin' Wild,* a black revue.

Another Lincoln film, *The Realization of a Negro's Ambition* (ca.

3. *By Right of Birth* was typical of black genre film in its portrayal of positive images as middle-class success figures. (George P. Johnson Collection, Research Library, UCLA)

1917) recast the Horatio Alger legend in black terms. *The Trooper of Troop K* (ca. 1920) recounted the yarn of the rough western loner, played by Noble Johnson, who, carrying a pure heart under his saddle dust and army blues, proves his goodness and wins the girl after fighting in a reenactment of a famous cavalry battle with Mexican marauders in the Southwest.

The marketing efforts of both the *Birth of a Race* Company and the Lincoln Motion Picture Company revealed the hazards of distributing movies outside established Hollywood channels. Hollywood had become an oligopoly that controlled almost all aspects of American filmmaking. All independent companies, whether "B" producers on Hollywood's "poverty row," Yiddish moviemakers in Manhattan, or race movie makers, suffered from both a lack of capital and outlets for sufficient distribution. Their finished films generally ran only in small second-run "grind" houses which owed no scheduling obligations to the large theater chains that were the backbone of Hollywood profits. At both ends of the production line, the economic structure threatened independent filmmakers with either loss of control or actual extinction. The Johnsons' inventive but eventually unsuccessful solution employed a string of black newspapermen, who both plugged their movies and acted as bookers.

Rather than holding out the promise of another stride toward a black genre, the next stage of black filmmaking revealed a negative aspect of making race movies. The Ebony Motion Picture of Chicago, like a number of other small white companies, produced films for black audiences behind a facade of black managers. But apparently their white "angels" and Southern white writer, Leslie T. Peacock, insisted on films like *A Black Sherlock Holmes* (ca. 1918) that were mere mirror images of white movies. Ebony's *Spying the Spy* (1919), for example, employed a talented black comedian in the role of an American spy in pursuit of a stereotyped German agent; the film's climax was an orgy of editorial effects which played upon the old-fashioned notion of the Afro-American fear of ghosts. While many blacks had migrated to cities, surprisingly, little of urban black life appeared on the screen. Furthermore, interest in foreign exotica had declined into a cycle of Edgar Rice Burroughs's Tarzan with its African supernumeraries. Revived by the coming of sound, blackface roles persisted.

Before 1925, strong black roles were brought to the screen by a corps of black Hollywood regulars in a handful of films that touched some unconscious truth about American racial life. Madame Sul-te-Wan, Onest Conley, Carolynne Snowden, Nathan Curry, Zach Williams, Raymond Turner, and boxers Sam Baker and George Godfrey brought conviction to these few roles. Noble Johnson typified their accomplishment and captivity by white Hollywood. His career spanned from World War I with Lubin, to a job as the Indian hothead, Red Shirt, in John Ford's *She Wore a Yellow Ribbon* (1949). Because his work with the Lincoln Motion Picture Company competed with the movies produced by his white employer, Universal Pictures, Johnson was asked to give up his work at Lincoln. Thereafter, through World War I, not only did he continue as a stock heavy in Universal's various "B" western series, *Red Feather, Red Ace,* and *Bull's Eye,* but went on to appear as scores of Indians, Latins, Asians, and primitive tribesmen in such movies as *Robinson Crusoe* (1917), *Leopard Woman* (1920), *Kismet* (1920), *The Four Horsemen of the Apocalypse* (1921) (in which he was one of the mounted plagues), *The Ten Commandments* (1923), *Flaming Frontier* (1926), *Aloma of the South Seas* (1926), *Ben Hur* (1927), and *Lady of the Harem* (1926). In some years he appeared in a half dozen or more pictures, ranging from major "epics" to routine "programmers."

The other source of strong black characterizations appeared in white movies in an indirect, muted way that barely hinted at the fact that American society had begun to deal with a new Negro who had migrated to Northern cities. In 1916 Bert Williams, the distinguished black comedian of the Ziegfeld Follies, appeared in *Fish* and *A Natural Born Gambler,* two movies that used blackface routines in a fresh way. In the former Williams was a gangling country boy, who tries to sell a fish as it grows stale. In *A Natural Born Gambler* he presides over the card table at his fraternal lodge while contriving to elude the white police. In the same period, Vitagraph made two parodies of white boxers whose fear of Jack Johnson formed the basis of comedy—*Some White Hope* (1915) and *The Night I Fought Jack Johnson* (1913). A black confidante far shrewder and more knowing than the Civil War cycle maids appeared in *Hoodoo Ann* (1916). Aggressive and even derisive black women appeared in Cecil B. DeMille's *Manslaughter* (1922). Several children's series that set the mood for the debut of Hal Roach's egalitarian *Our Gang* began in the late 1920s. The variety of black roles expanded to include French and American soldiers, wise old boxing trainers, horse trainers, and a number of servants who resembled Tonto, the Lone Ranger's sidekick, more than they did Rastus, the ante-bellum butler.

Despite their contribution to the wearing away of old icons that had symbolized the former inferior status of Afro-Americans, these deviations from ancient norms spoke little of the "new Negro" who was already celebrated in Northeastern literary circles. If white moviemakers understandably failed to take into account the changed circumstances of urban blacks, their black counterparts also failed to fill the existing void. Nor did a growing number of black critics suggest new images to replace the outdated ones, except for a vague plea for presenting "positive"—meaning middle-class—characters on the screen.

But the condition of the "new Negro" was not that clearcut. As Afro-Americans moved from Southern farms to Northern cities, they fell prey to oppressive forces from outside the group. Their plight may be likened to that of the Germans, described in an essay by Erich Kahler (1974). In the Middle Ages, Germans, like blacks, spoke a language built upon linguistic traditions from outside the group; lived in rural regions and disdained the city or found it alien; embraced millenial ideals rather than small victories; and chose in-group stratification as a means of preserving the group, despite anarchic forces pressing from the outside. Moreover, in the face of these external forces, whether Frankish kings in Paris, Italian condottieri in the pay of the Pope, or Magyar invaders, the Germans often responded with in-group aggression.

The wide gulf between white movies and black aspirations may be seen in a fragmentary glance at some of D.W. Griffith's 1920s films. After the release of *The Birth of a Nation,* Griffith went on to make several masterpieces such as *Intolerance* (1916), *Broken Blossoms* (1919), *Way Down East* (1920), and *Orphans of the Storm* (1921). Like most of his works, these films commented on social issues from the safe vantage point of the past or foreign locales. In the mid-1920s, however, Griffith addressed himself to modern times.

Here Griffith's racial vision, like that of most of his white countrymen, was unable to distinguish rural blacks from the new urban Negro. The black characters in *One Exciting Night* (1922) were strikingly off the mark. The central character, an improbable detective, was a "Kaffir, the dark terror of the bootleg gang." The remaining black roles were played by blackfaced whites as traditional servile flunkies, who trailed through the plot. A year later in *The White Rose* (1923), Griffith attempted to return to Southern ground, but his critics leapt upon him for his "mawkish sickening sentimentality" and his "jumbled and pointless plot." According to them, he seemed a "genius out of touch with the world." Next he began *His Darker Self* (1924), another blackface picture starring Al Jolson, who eventually deserted the project. Still later Griffith made an unsatisfying and fruitless appearance on the set of Universal's *Topsy and Eva* (1927), an exploitation spinoff from that studio's successful *Uncle Tom's Cabin.* In every case these were "white" movies, retailing Negroes almost as an in-group joke.

At last in the mid-1920s black critics on black newspapers, among them Lester Walton of the New York *Age,* Romeo Daugherty of the *Amsterdam News,* J. A. Rogers, and D. Ireland Thomas, began to develop a common vision. A few white papers also developed a racial sensitivity; in particular, *Variety* crowed in glee when the Ku

Klux Klan muddled a filmmaking project. When promoters gave a press preview for a racist tract called *Free and Equal* (1925), *Variety* howled: "it is not only old fashioned but so crudely done that the Sunday night audience laughed it practically out of the theater."

But neither Griffith nor the press provided the fairest gauge of Hollywood's inability to deal with black themes. Rather, it was the mixed response that blacks gave to the best and most well-meaning Hollywood movie, Universal's *Uncle Tom's Cabin*. In 1926 Carl Laemmle started the project by signing Charles Gilpin, the most distinguished black actor of his day, to play Tom. However, Gilpin was soon replaced by James Lowe, who gave one of the finest black cinema performances in a faithful rendering of the spirit of Harriet Beecher Stowe's novel.

Unfortunately for Laemmle, black critics and audiences alike split in their judgment of the film that had been aimed at a "cross-over" audience of blacks and whites, who would like either its abolitionism or its nostalgia. But no amount of mere preaching on the subject of race satisfied those blacks who looked to film as a medium for communicating to a black audience.

Nevertheless, in comparison with the films of the early 1920s, blacks saw in *Uncle Tom's Cabin* a new Hollywood that seemed to promise a fair representation of black characters, liberal progress, and cause for hope. One producer promised a movie of the new Broadway hit, *Porgy* (1927); John M. Stahl put a serious black love scene in *In Old Kentucky* (1927); William Wellman's hopeful *Beggars of Life* featured a fine role by Edgar "Blue" Washington; DeMille's *Old Ironsides* (1926) carried a crew that included strong black roles, as did Alan Crosland's *The Sea Beast* (1926); and Monta Bell's *Man, Woman, and Sin* (1927) established its urban milieu with neat vignettes of black city life.

In the absence of movies that spoke directly to black concerns, a kind of black underground grew outside the major studios. Although largely white-owned, it nonetheless attempted to reach the black audience that was untouched by Hollywood. Strapped by poor distribution channels, paltry budgets, amateurish actors, technical failings, and untrained crews, these production companies were somehow able to release films for black audiences throughout the silent era. Their films reached beyond mere representation of Negroes on the screen to depict Afro-Americans as a presence in American life.

Most of these race movie makers felt an obligation to present blacks as icons of virtue and honor. One case in point, the Douglass Company of New Jersey, used war film heroism "to show the better side of 'Negro life' " and to "inspire in the Negro a desire to climb higher." They also adapted films from the works of popular Negro authors such as Paul Laurence Dunbar's *The Scapegoat* (1917). Another Douglass project, *The Colored American Winning His Suit* (1916), followed the career of the Negro hero who was "getting ahead." Other companies turned War Department films into *From Harlem to the Rhine* (ca. 1918), *Our Hell Fighters Return* (1919), anl other compilations showing black troops in combat.

By the early 1920s the New York *Age* headlined that COLORED MOTION PICTURES ARE IN GREAT DEMAND. The filmmakers were undaunted by any topic; the whole black world was their stage, and their regional roots gave a varied flavor to the black experience they recorded on film. This excitement stirred still other prospective producers to grind out glossy prospectuses that promised great black films which would never be made. Their known films included the Norman Company's all-black westerns shot in the famous all-black town of Boley, Oklahoma, starring the New York actress Anita Bush. The Cotton Blossom Company and the Lone Star Company made similar pictures in San Antonio. Dr. A. Porter Davis made *The Lure of a Woman* (1921), the first film produced in Kansas City.

After 1922, the Renaissance Company made black newsreels. White producers like Ben Strasser and Robert Levy (whose Reol Company made a movie from Dunbar's *Sport of the Gods* [1921]) joined the ranks of race movie makers. War movies persisted as a

4. Race movies provided the only vehicle through which black authors
could reach the screen. Dunbar's work, *The Sport of the Gods,* appeared in 1921. (George P. Johnson Collection, Research Library,
UCLA)

genre. Among these, Sidney P. Dones's *Injustice* (1920) was a wartime tale of Negroes and the Red Cross; two others, *Democracy, Or a Fight for Right* (1919) and *Loyal Hearts* (1919), "a smashing Virile Story of Our Race Heroes," were released by the Democracy Photoplay Corporation.

The most dogged of the race movie makers was Oscar Micheaux. Micheaux, a young black who had been a homesteader on the Dakota prairie, survived nearly twenty-five years in a desperately cutthroat business, turning out approximately two dozen movies in Chicago, New York, and New Jersey. As early as 1919, Micheaux tried unsuccessfully to link up with the Lincoln Company, a union that failed because the Johnsons considered him an upstart, a mountebank, and an untrustworthy hustler—ironically all traits that would help him achieve success.

Micheaux's production style gave texture to black genre films even if his work was not noted for its excellence of cinematic technique. To make up for a lack of technical expertise his black and white casts and crews exhibited a fellowship that blended the ideals of African tribal communities with the like values of a typical John Ford stock company of the 1940s. Ford's people shared the dust, cursed the heat, and passed the whiskey bottle together, thereby giving an unmistakeable Ford quality to their films. Micheaux never shot a film in the desert, but his companies, by sharing poverty, late paychecks, and shabby working conditions, somehow managed to give a generic texture to their films.

In like manner, Micheaux's shooting in idle and antique studios in Chicago, Fort Lee, and the Bronx; the jarring effect of the uneven talents of his actors; his use of unsung, under-employed white cameramen abandoned by the drift of filmmaking to Hollywood; and his shoestring operation which reflected the cast's own lives, all lent the enterprise an aura of outlawry. By merely finishing a film, Micheaux's company was like the legendary tricksters of black folklore, who win the game against the system. Thus the low pay, borrowed equipment, and nagging debtors helped define the character of the completed movie.

The difference between Micheaux and the other producers of the black genre can be compared to the difference between Orson Welles and Irving Thalberg. Welles was the outsider, flippant and contemptuous of established custom; Thalberg was the middle-class company man, loyal to MGM until his dying day, who succeeded by not offending either boss or audience. Micheaux, like Welles, had the gall to be opinionated in the presence of more experienced filmmakers. Welles once described his studio facilities as the finest Erector set a boy could ever hope for. Like Welles from his vantage point outside the system, Micheaux may have experienced a similar feeling of raw, fey power over the conventional filmmaking regime.

Motion pictures gave Micheaux the power to say, however amateurishly, what no other Negro filmmakers even thought of saying. He filmed the unnameable, arcane, disturbing things that set black against black. When others sought only uplifting and positive images, Micheaux searched for ironies.

A recurring theme appeared in his work from his very first film in 1919. The autobiographical *The Homesteader* recounted the story of a farm boy torn between rural values and urban glitter, a vehicle later used by Richard Wright in *Native Son* and Ralph Ellison in *The Invisible Man*. In this film, the conflict between the values of Southern black migrants to the city and the urbane sensibility that had scant room for enthusiastic religion, filiopietism, and the pride of land ownership, was examined.

Save for his densely packed polemic against jackleg preachers, *Body and Soul,* Oscar Micheaux's silent films are lost. But surviving reviews indicate that Micheaux was capable of an arrogant variety of themes, each one bringing some corner of Negro life to the screen. Indeed, he explored even white life as it impinged upon blacks—a rarity in race movies. His movies formed an anatomy of black filmmaking by the breadth of their topicality. In *Within Our Gates* (1920), Micheaux reconstructed an anti-Semitic lynching he had witnessed in Atlanta. *The Brute* (1925) starred black boxer Sam Langford. *The Symbol of the Unconquered* (1921) indicted the Ku Klux Klan at the height of its Middle Western revival.

Oscar Micheaux's
WITHIN OUR GATES
A Story of the Negro

5. More than any other maker of race movies, Oscar Micheaux brought social issues to the screen. *Within Our Gates* purported to be based on an eyewitness account of a lynching.

Birthright (1924) adapted T. S. Stribling's novel about the racism that blighted the life of a black Harvard graduate. *The Spider's Web* (1927) dramatized the ghetto's love-hate affair with the infamous gambling system, the numbers game. With the release of *The Conjure Woman* (1926) and *The House Behind the Cedars* (1927), Micheaux revealed his most unabashed nerve by persuading the distinguished black novelist, Charles Waddell Chesnutt, not only to sell the movie rights to two of his books for a few dollars, but also to tolerate Micheaux's heavy-handed rewriting.

Sadly, only *Body and Soul,* the lone survivor of Micheaux's early films, reveals the quality of his silent work. Although flawed by censors' efforts, *Body and Soul* made use of the young and marginally employed football player, singer, budding actor, and preacher's son, Paul Robeson, to make a strong case against venal preachers. This film helped make Micheaux a central figure in black genre film, if for no other reason than he willingly, even sensationally, assaulted black problems. In addition, he brought black fiction to the screen, criticized American racial custom, and made his own migratory life an allegory for the black experience in the twentieth century.

Parallel to Micheaux's career in the 1920s, another variant of black genre film producers emerged: the company rich in white capital, technical capacity, and leadership, with a self-conscious ambition to present films that reflected the lives of its Negro audiences. Unlike their competitors who ground out shabby black mimics of white life, this enterprising group of easterners kept a keen ear tuned to black circles and a sharp eye on box office trends as sensors of black taste. In the early 1920s, the best of them, theater owner Robert Levy, a backer of the Lafayette Players black theatre group, founded Reol as a studio that intended to produce such films as Chesnutt's *The Marrow of Tradition.*

Still another white force was the owner whose theater gradually had turned "colored" and who subsequently made films for the new audiences. On the eve of sound film, such a group led by David Starkman and a white studio crew united behind Sherman "Uncle Dud" Dudley, a black vaudevillian and impresario from Washington. The resulting Colored Players Company produced its first film by July 1926, *A Prince of His Race,* a melodrama on the theme of the black bourgeois fear of lost status. By the end of the year they released a black version of the old temperance tract, *Ten Nights in a Bar Room,* starring Charles Gilpin. Far from a rehash, the brief film used its all-black cast to achieve a certain poignancy, as though the actors themselves were making a special plea to urban blacks, warning them against urban vices in a manner reminiscent of Micheaux.

In 1928 the Colored Players Company achieved its finest hour with *The Scar of Shame,* which, in the wrong hands, might have become no more than a sentimental "women's picture." In style, mood, and theme, however, the Colored Players' film brought a sophisticated close to the silent film era. Scriptwriter David Starkman, two Italian collaborators, director Frank Perugini and cameraman Al Ligouri, and black stars Lucia Lynn Moses, Harry Henderson, Lawrence Chenault, and Pearl McCormick, combined efforts to produce a wistful satire on the color caste system that stratified urban black society. The completed film went beyond its premise by adding a commentary on the American success myth. Perhaps because authors can most successfully romanticize or satirize what they know from a distance, as in Samuel Taylor Coleridge's *Xanadu,* J. M. W. Turner's painting of a shimmering man-o-war in the tow of a steam tug, or J. R. R. Tolkien's *Middle Earth,* the largely white Colored Players sympathetically exposed an anomaly in black life—Negroes, the victims of racial discrimination, sometimes stratified into fraternities, professions, marriages, and even churches along lines denoted by skin color.

The boom of the 1920s ended sadly for Afro-Americans. The Great Depression proved a shattering experience, hitting blacks sooner and more severely than it did whites. Even the Republican party cast them aside in Herbert Hoover's so-called "lily white" convention of 1928.

And yet, the sound film era began at the same time, holding out the promise of revolutionary change for blacks in Hollywood. MGM and Fox stumbled over each other trying to exploit sound film through the use of Negro themes and motifs. These studios were so successful that their work instigated the gradual turning away of black film audiences from race movies, toward Hollywood.

Although Christie Comedies had once used Spencer Williams as a writer, for the first time Hollywood producers really made use of black consultants. MGM's *Hallelujah!* benefitted from the counsel of Harold Garrison, the studio bootblack, and James Weldon Johnson of the NAACP. Fox's *Hearts in Dixie,* like the MGM film, brought black religion, tragedy, music, and emotion to the screen with the help of Clarence Muse and other blacks on the set.

Immediately a rash of musical shorts emerged from the studios. The worst of them, such as Christie's comedies, were based on Octavus Roy Cohen's old *Saturday Evening Post* dialect stories. The best of them used black performers in ways that allowed them to influence the ambience of the films. Aubrey Lyles and Flournoy Miller, the comedy team from the original *Shuffle Along* revue of 1921, the dancing Covans, the Hall Johnson Choir, baritone Jules Bledsoe, Duke Ellington, and many others were signed by Hollywood studios.

The best of these appeared early in the decade. Louis Armstrong and Cab Calloway infused a strong jazz beat into *I'll Be Glad When You're Dead, You Rascal You* (1932), *Minnie the Moocher* (1932), *Rhapsody in Black and Blue* (1932), and *Jitterbug Party* (1935). Eubie Blake and Noble Sissle enlivened *Pie Pie Blackbird* (ca. 1932). The Nicholas Brothers brought their jazz acrobatics to *Barbershop Blues* (1933) and *The Black Network* (1936). Jimmy Mordecai, one of the greatest jazz dancers, did a stylized, moody rendering of Southern folk life in *Yamacraw* (1930). These films continued until World War II when Lena Horne, Teddy Wilson, Albert Ammons, and Pete Johnson did a musical fantasy of the disinherited, *Boogie Woogie Dream* (1944).

The most balanced combinations of mood, lighting, music, black social themes, and theatrical elements were offered in Duke Ellington's *Symphony in Black* (1935) and *Black and Tan* (1929). *Symphony* was scored in four movements with stylized bits of black history cut to match the beat of work songs, chants, and fervent religious moods. The film's ending featured Billie Holiday and Earl "Snakehips" Tucker in an urban scene that symbolized Negro migration from Africa, to the South, to Harlem, to modern times. Almost ritual in form, the film demonstrated the possibilities of black art emerging from a Hollywood factory. In like manner *Black and Tan* recreated a similar ambience but stressed plot more than music by focusing on Ellington's woman, who, despite poor health, dances so that he might finish his composition; but she dies on the dance floor, a martyr to black music. Both films were effectively heightened

6. During the Harlem Renaissance, black genre works often were influenced by white intellectuals. Here Dudley Murphy, Duke Ellington, and Carl Van Vechten (left to right) confer on the set of *Black and Tan*. (International Museum of Photography, George Eastman House)

by chiaroscuro lighting of a quality that seldom graced feature movies.

A few musical films made outside Hollywood provided still more promising avenues of black expression within the context of a medium dominated by whites. The best single case is Dudley Murphy's *The St. Louis Blues* (1928). Its gritty black mood emanated from the musical contributions of W.C. Handy, Jimmy Mordecai, J. Rosamond Johnson, and Bessie Smith. It was as though Murphy served only as a neutral vehicle which carried the black imagery to the screen.

Five years later, another combination of cinematically inexperienced blacks joined Murphy to produce a unique film version of Eugene O'Neill's *The Emperor Jones* (1933). O'Neill's play mixed psychological depth with racial grotesques through the treatment of a black hero, who aimed beyond traditionally accepted black channels of endeavor. Murphy's film became an instrument through which white writers, and black musicians and performers combined to construct a black film. Paul Robeson, Fredi Washington, and Frank Wilson starred in the black roles and Rosamond Johnson scored the music, using traditional black themes, motifs, and styles.

Many Hollywood movies that followed treated Negroes with awareness if not sensibility, with politesse if not equality, and affection if not understanding. Nevertheless, these films of the depression years amounted to a quantum jump from the old-fashioned racial metaphors of the previous decade. These gestures toward a liberalized cinema promised enough to attract larger black audiences into 1930s movie palaces. As a result, during the Great Depression, producers of race movies lost ground to their Hollywood adversaries. The black press, motivated by increased studio and theater advertising and loyalty to black actors, cheered the trend. In contrast to the Hollywood product, race movie makers appeared more than ever as inept, erratic mavericks.

The trendy black images ranged broadly, if not deeply. Lewis Milestone's *Hallelujah, I'm a Bum* (1933) featured a black hobo

7. The marshalling of black creative forces outside of Hollywood allowed the commanding presence of Paul Robeson (right), here with Dudley Digges, to come to the screen as *The Emperor Jones*. (© United Artists)

among its down-and-outers. A cycle of exposés of horrible prison conditions featured black prisoners. Etta Moten and Ivie Anderson sang important songs in *Gold Diggers of 1933, Flying Down to Rio* (1933), and *A Day at the Races* (1937). Louis Armstrong and Martha Raye's raucous interracial number in *Artists and Models* (1937) shocked southern censors. Stepin Fetchit, the archfoe of the black bourgeoisie, worked steadily, though with ever narrowing range. Following a trend set by MGM's *Trader Horn* (1931), the worst painted-savage stereotypes faded from major movies, although they continued to survive in the "B" pictures shot on the backlots of "poverty row." A few movies depicted the South in unflattering terms and its Negroes as less than happy with their lot. Among these were *Cabin in the Cotton* (1932), *I Was a Fugitive from a Chain Gang* (1932), *Slave Ship, Jezebel* (1938), and *The Little Foxes* (1941). Black boon companions grew more humane in *Dirigible* (1931), *Broadway Bill* (1934), *O'Shaughnessy's Boy* (1937), *Prestige* (1932), *The Count of Monte Cristo* (1934), and especially *Massacre* (1934). A few genuinely fine roles appeared: Clarence Brooks's Haitian doctor in John Ford's *Arrowsmith,* Fredi Washington's wistful mulattoes in *Imitation of Life* (1934) and *One Mile from Heaven* (1937), Muse's angry rebel and Daniel Haynes's big-house butler in *So Red the Rose,* Hattie McDaniel's prickly servants in *Alice Adams* (1935), *The Mad Miss Manton* (1938), and *Gone with the Wind* (1939), and Clinton Rosamond's outraged father in *Golden Boy* (1939).

A sample taken from twenty months at mid-decade reveals the broad sweep of change in Hollywood Negro roles during the New Deal. Despite the changing times, some traditional roles persisted. Old Southern legends were faithfully served by Bill Robinson's dancing servants in *The Little Colonel* (1935) and *The Littlest Rebel,* along with nostalgic relics such as Edward Sutherland's *Mississippi* (1935). Stepin Fetchit's career reached high gear in a string of Fox's celebrations of rural folk life such as *Steam Boat Round the Bend* (1935), *David Harum* (1934), *Judge Priest* (1934), and *The County Chairman* (1934). *Bullets or Ballots* (1936) and *Hooray for Love* (1935) brought Negroes into urban contexts through Louise Beavers's "numbers' queen" and Bill Robinson's street-dandy. John Ford's *The Prisoner of Shark Island* (1936) depicted black soldiers as well as slaves. A few Broadway successes brought strong black roles to Hollywood intact, among them Edward Thompson's "Slim" in *The Petrified Forest* (1936), Leigh Whipper's "Crooks" in John Steinbeck's *Of Mice and Men* (1939), and Rex Ingram's "De Lawd" and "Hezdrel" roles in Marc Connelly's fable of black folk religion, *The Green Pastures* (a less than total success among black critics). Universal's remake of *Showboat*

8. *The Petrified Forest* was one of dozens of films made during the Great Depression that competed with race movies by reflecting a trend toward more significant black roles. Here Edward Thompson as "Slim" (right) is part of Duke Mantee's (Humphrey Bogart) outlaw band. (© Warner Brothers)

(1936) brought "Joe" to the screen in the person of Paul Robeson. And Fritz Lang and Mervyn LeRoy made indictments of lynching, *Fury* (1936) and *They Won't Forget* (1937), although each was weakened by placing blacks on the periphery rather than depicting them as victims of mobs.

Black critics and audiences waffled. On the one hand they were happy to see more blacks on the screen, but on the other, they fretted over Hollywood's superficiality and its ignorance of black life.

David O. Selznick's *Gone with the Wind* grew into the media event most symptomatic of black division over the merits of a Hollywood movie. Nominally a film version of Margaret Mitchell's overweight novel of the South during Reconstruction, the movie quickly developed a split personality. Selznick was torn between the conflicting goals of wishing to accommodate to liberal political trends by having (according to a memorandum) "the Negroes come out decidedly on the right side of the ledger," at the same time that he was striving for historicity and genuine Southern ambience. To achieve this all but impossible ambition, Selznick hired experts —Atlanta architect, artist, and antiquarian Wilbur G. Kurtz and Susan Myrick of the *Macon Telegraph*— to authenticate details of regional atmosphere and racial etiquette. They saved the film from countless errors of manners, accents, and clichés, such as warning the company against having the slaves rise in song; in the latter episode, they worked in cooperation with Hall Johnson, the black choirmaster. From the North, writers Sidney Howard, Ben Hecht, O.H.P. Garrett, and F. Scott Fitzgerald, in deference to modern tastes, elided references to the Ku Klux Klan and depictions of the Yankee army as marauders and looters. The hoped-for result, Selznick felt, would be that authentic black maids, mammies, and field hands were considerably more humanized than those appearing in earlier Southern genre films.

Despite its brilliance as a work of popular art, *Gone with the Wind* inspired both black praise and calumny, revealing a still unsatisfied hunger for a black genre cinema. On one side many urban blacks agreed with a *Pittsburgh Courier* critic who found that "much of it was distasteful to the Negro race." On the other, Bill Chase of the *Amsterdam News* responded with exaggerated disbelief. "Ye gads, what's happening to Hollywood?" he wrote. Several writers focused on the black acting, especially that of Hattie McDaniel, who made mammy "more than a servant" and won an Oscar. She tipped still more black opinion in favor of the movie.

This is not to say *Gone with the Wind* revolutionized Hollywood into a center of black genre filmmaking. Yet, the film stood astride two epochs. In the period between the wars, black roles had slowly moved away from tradition. With the coming of World War II, the liberal drift became part of the rhetoric of Allied war aims.

Gone with the Wind admirably expressed the tension between the two poles of racial ideals—tradition and change—with the result that on the eve of World War II, Afro-Americans responded to cinema in two distinct ways, both of them new departures from convention. They tempered their customary cynical view of Hollywood with a renewed faith in their own ability to change Hollywood through social and political pressure. Perhaps as a result, many black filmmakers lost direction and affiliated with white "angels." Micheaux joined first with Frank Schiffman, then with Jack Goldberg. William Alexander affiliated with Emmanuel Glucksman; Spencer Williams with Alfred Sack; George Randol and Ralph Cooper with Harry Popkin; and so on.

Thus by the late 1930s independent filmmakers reawakened interest in black genre by simply recreating Hollywood genres, i.e., gangster movies infused with black cops, crooks, judges, and jailers. Where the first generation of black filmmakers had examined black social issues, the new crop, including many whites, focused on tried and proven Hollywood genre formulas recast in black form, with an admixture of racial awareness. Thus, on the eve of World War II, more than ever black film would be identified by its content more than technique. Like the western and the gangster film, black genre emerged from a melding of legendary, ritual themes, aspiration, solidarity, and pride, set in immediately identifiable locales.

Exceptions to the trend were the expatriates Paul Robeson and Josephine Baker. Baker, who had gone to Paris in a chorus line in the 1920s, became a sensation in the Folies Bergère. Eventually she turned up in a string of exotic primitive roles in such vehicles as *The Siren of the Tropics* (1928), *Princess Tam-Tam* (ca. 1938), and *Zou-Zou* (ca. 1935), all of which failed, in the words of one critic, because her work "renders the Negro ignoble." While Robeson was more thoughtful in choosing roles, he was rarely more successful. Most of his British movies celebrated sentimental working class comradeship, African folklore, and British colonialism with equal vigor. *King Solomon's Mines* (1937), *Sanders of the River* (1935),

9. Obscured by the success of *Gone With the Wind*, *Way Down South* pioneered by giving credits to black writers Langston Hughes and Clarence Muse. (© RKO; National Film Archive, London)

10. Overseas films contributed little to black genres. Josephine Baker's exotic primitive movies such as *The Flame of Paris* differed only marginally from Hollywood stereotypes. (Hoffberg Productions)

Jericho (1937), *Proud Valley* (1940) —each exploited his presence while avoiding his politics. The void in Hollywood and abroad left the field to the independent race movie makers.

However, economic stress had driven some black producers, among them Micheaux, into bankruptcy and resulting dependence upon white money. After 1931, blacks raised capital from Frank Schiffman of Harlem's Apollo Theatre, Robert Levy of Reol, and white Southern distributors like Ted Toddy and Alfred Sack. By the end of the decade, the Goldberg brothers, Arthur Dreifuss, Edgar G. Ulmer, Arthur Hoerle, Emmanuel Glucksman, Harry and Leo Popkin, Robert Savini, Ben Rinaldo, and Jed Buell, all white, prevailed.

The new generation of race movies revived interest in the genre precisely because they were like Hollywood movies. Although they seemed less black, these films did try to include blacks in the American myth, through inclusion of the total subculture, rather than integration of individuals. Because the films crackled with black heroes, heavies, cops, grifters, boxers, and scientists, the black audiences could claim the right to these roles in real life.

Not since the 1920s had black critics held such high hopes for race movies. Early Depression movies had been bad, including Micheaux's *Ten Minutes to Live* (1932), *The Girl from Chicago* (1932), and *The Exile* (1931); Rosebud's *Absent* (1931); Harry Gant's *Georgia Rose* (1931); Donald Heywood's parody of Garveyism, *The Black King* (1933); and Robert Mintz's and Louis Weiss's *Drums O'Voodoo* (1933), the first movie based on the work of a black dramatist, J. Augustus Smith.

But by 1938 technically competent whites directed black actors in a manner similar to that of a "B" picture assembly line. Gangster films like Ulmer's *Moon over Harlem* (1939) and Dreifuss's *Murder on Lenox Avenue* (1941) combined studio proficiency with a black social message, calling for sacrifice and solidarity. Only Micheaux and Spencer Williams wrestled with their white "angels" for control. Labor usually divided along the lines of white enterprise and black creativity. On the West Coast, for example, Million Dollar Pictures formed around white Hollywoodians Harry and Leo Popkin, black actor Ralph Cooper, and black director George Randol. The gangster subgenre included *Dark Manhattan* (1937), *Gang War* (ca. 1938), *Bargain with Bullets* (1937), *Underworld* (1937), *Mystery in Swing* (1938), and *Double Deal* (1939). In a fair example, Ralph Cooper played a doctor torn between a decision to patch up crooks or to open a free medical clinic in Harlem.

A small western subgenre including *Harlem Rides the Range* (1939), *Bronze Buckaroo* (1938), *Two Gun Man from Harlem* (1939), and *Harlem on the Prairie* (1938) combined a black mythic hero, Herb Jeffries, as a singing cowboy with the blackface routines of Flournoy Miller and Mantan Moreland. Sports autobiography was another briefly popular subgenre. Ty Cobb, Jack Dempsey, Babe Ruth and other athletes had made such movies. But these could not match *Keep Punching* (1939) and *Spirit of Youth* (1937), the "bios" of black champions Henry Armstrong and Joe Louis, respectively. In particular, Louis's religiosity and intense shyness brought the metier of boxing across on film.

On the eve of World War II, race movies marched awkwardly out of step with liberal war aims. Afro-Americans and liberal whites shared with international allies a "popular front" against Fascist racism. Race movies seemed to be reactionary vestiges of past oppression. Marxists picketed Micheaux's *God's Step Children* (1938) because it "slandered Negroes, holding them up to ridicule." The black press condemned Mantan Moreland's Dixie National film, *Mr. Washington Goes to Town* (1940), as "undignified," in the mildest of many assaults on the genre.

Micheaux made one last attempt to return to independent black roots. Along with Colonel Hubert Julian, the "black eagle" who had sought to duplicate Lindbergh's flight, Micheaux attempted to produce a pair of black-financed melodramas. But after a disastrous premiere in New York dutifully attended by white politicians and celebrities, the genre lapsed into a wartime coma, followed by Micheaux's final film, a few Goldberg and Toddy releases, a few of William Alexander's All-America films, and a rush of Louis Jordan musicals.

The race movies had no place in the war years' optimistic integrationism. The NAACP called its national convention in Hollywood, in 1942, to make new demands. Walter White, the Executive Secretary, counsel Wendell Willkie, the recently defeated Republican presidential candidate, and several liberal Hollywood whites agreed to improve the quality and quantity of black roles and to expand opportunities in the studio crafts. *Variety* ran the page one story headed BETTER BREAKS FOR NEGROES IN H'WOOD. Unfortunately for race movie makers, the plans backfired, smothering

11. By the end of the 1930s, race movies like Million Dollar's *While Thousands Cheer* exploited famous athletes and performers, rather than pressing social issues.

black movies save for "soundies," the sixteen millimeter films made for jukeboxes by black Ivy League football star, Fritz Pollard, and a handful of others.

In the early 1940s many Hollywood Negro roles took on touches of dignity, courage, and humanity, a trend that was given modest direction by the NAACP agreement. The servants in Lillian Hellman's *The Little Foxes* were like griots of family lore. The plot of *In This Our Life* (1942) turned on the fate of a young black law student. Much of the mood of *Casablanca* (1942) was set by Dooley Wilson's "Sam." Each of the war dramas, *Sahara, Crash Dive, Bataan,* and *Lifeboat,* all made in 1943, placed a Negro in the fight against Fascism. William Wellman's film of Walter Van Tilburg Clark's *The Ox Bow Incident* (1943) included Leigh Whipper

12. During World War II, the international struggle against Fascism stirred a liberal trend that racially integrated the United States Navy on film many years before official policy introduced integration to the troops. In *Crash Dive,* Benny Carter (right) is in the front rank of an amphibious assault. (© 20th Century-Fox; Nederlands Stichting Film-museum)

among the victims of a lynching. *Mission to Moscow* (1943) featured Whipper as Haile Selassie, while *Stormy Weather* focused on another historical figure, bandmaster Jim Europe. MGM's *Cabin in the Sky* was an all-black musical. At least six Army training films attempted to deal with racial problems in the military.

The extent of changes in wartime racial attitudes is seen in the black response to two 1940s films that might have been lauded for efforts in social progress in the 1930s. Instead, Walt Disney's *Song of the South* (1946) and Julien Duvivier's *Tales of Manhattan* (1942) brought down the wrath of organized Negroes because of their whimsically old-fashioned roles played by James Baskette and Paul Robeson.

The black genre in the 1940s survived only in documentary film. From the days of World War I combat footage by the Signal Corps to the New Deal, the government had done little with film. Commercial producers had limited their work to pseudo-anthropological jungle films or, like the prestigious *March of Time,* sensationalist exposés of voodoo in Harlem and acrobatic Lindy Hoppers at the Harvest Moon Ball. During World War II, however, the War Department chose film as the medium for explaining to the troops *Why We Fight.* Among the projects, a training film, *The Negro Soldier,* fell to a young black filmmaker, Carlton Moss.

A well-constructed celebration of the contribution of Afro-Americans to their country's military history, *The Negro Soldier* was applauded by black journalists and went into commercial release under the auspices of the Office of War Information. The war years' liberalism eventually inspired a minor cycle of government films; among them *The Negro College in Wartime* (ca. 1944), *The Negro Sailor* (ca. 1944), and *Henry Brown, Farmer* (1943) are noteworthy for black contributions to them. The trend extended to Hollywood where Gjon Mili's *Jammin' the Blues* (1944), an evocative jazz documentary, was *Life's* "Movie of the Week."

By the age of integration, roughly between 1947 and 1965, black film identity blended with a general American identity. The heroes were Sidney Poitier, for his convincing portrayals of Negroes on the margin of white life, and Louis Armstrong, the perpetual ambassador to the white world. The period had grown out of the wartime exposure of the gap between American racial ideals and social facts. The liberal momentum of the war years continued in a postwar cycle of message movies in which bigotry was the heavy. *Lost Boundaries* (1949) examined Negroes who had "passed" into the white world; *Pinky* similarly traced a light-skinned girl's return to the black world; *Home of the Brave* (1949), shot in secret because of its volatile theme, observed the impact of racism on a black soldier's psyche; Clarence Brown's version of William Faulkner's *Intruder in the Dust* (1949) looked at racism from inside the white

13. After World War II, racial liberalism became so fashionable that Stanley Kramer rushed *Home of the Brave* into secret production in order to beat the competition. (© United Artists)

social conscience; *No Way Out* (1950) followed a race riot from the viewpoint of black victims; Harry and Leo Popkin's *The Well* (1951) showed how racism could polarize a village.

In the 1950s, as though blacks had been admitted to the mainstream of American life, movie themes emphasized individual attainment rather than group solidarity. No less than two film accounts of the Harlem Globetrotters appeared, along with *The Joe Louis Story* (1953) and *The Jackie Robinson Story* (1950). While Sidney Poitier's career ebbed and flowed, three incisive studies of race relations stood out: *Blackboard Jungle* (1955), *The Defiant Ones* (1958), and the moving *Lilies of the Field,* for which he won an

14. Because so much postwar film spoke for changing white politics rather than black hopes, Richard Wright took his own production unit abroad to make a personally controlled film version of his novel *Native Son*. Nevertheless, a fanciful dream sequence hindered the impact of the message. (© Classic Pictures; Library of Congress)

Oscar. Less successful was Darryl Zanuck's *Island in the Sun* (1957), which concealed rather than illuminated racial conflict. With uneven success, Hollywood tried to capture the black musical achievement on film in *Carmen Jones* (1954), *Porgy and Bess* (1959), and *Young Man with a Horn* (1950).

Black movies as a genre moved to the periphery of the industry in these twenty years of postwar liberalism. Richard Wright produced a film version of his novel, *Native Son* (1951), in Argentina, save for a few atmospheric shots of Chicago. Leroi Jones's (Imamu Baraka) *Dutchman* (1967) was completed in England because of the filmmaker's wish for freedom from constraints. Shirley Clarke's *The Cool World* (1964), a grainy street story set in black Harlem, found its main market in college rentals or as a retitled exploitation item. Marcel Camus's *Orfeu Negro* (1960) came from Brazil, and gave ominous new meaning to color. Larry Peerce's *One Potato, Two Potato* (1965), which managed to overcome the strictures of the message movie format, was infused with elements of black life, largely through sharply etched performances by Vinette Carroll and Robert Earl Jones. Among these social movies were a pair of stage successes: *Purlie Victorious* (1964) and Hansberry's *A Raisin in the Sun,* the former a broad satire on the old South, the latter a claustrophobic, real study of a black family strained by a move to suburbia. *To Kill a Mockingbird* (1962) was the best of several liberal morality tales. The tensions of the period were exploited by a substratum of contrivances that included Hugo Haas's *Night of the Quarter Moon* (1959), Stephen Borden's French import, *My Baby is Black* (1965), and Larry Buchanan's *Free, White, and 21* (1963).

Nevertheless, for black intellectuals and prospective filmmakers, the period held promise. Both the NAACP and federal agencies pressured studios into hiring Negroes. As a result, Afro-Americans entered the industry in greater numbers—Harry Belafonte in production, Wendell Franklin in direction, Quincy Jones in music, Vincent Tubbs in publicity. Also, blacks in ever increasing numbers began to appear in complex and varied roles, including Poitier's psychiatrist in *Pressure Point* (1962); Sammy Davis's hip inmate in *Convicts Four* (1962); Maidie Norman's rational maid in *What Ever Happened to Baby Jane?* (1962); the three or four dozen extras in *Kisses for My President* (1964); the stolid presence of Jim Brown; Poitier's reaching for breadth in *Lilies of the Field, The Long Ships* (1964), *The Organization* (1971), *The Lost Man* (1969), and in the ill-timed and therefore misjudged *Guess Who's Coming to Dinner* (1967); the toadies played by Sammy Davis and Woody Strode in *Sergeants Three* (1962) and *Two Rode Together* (1961), and John Ford's timid movie about the Buffalo Soldiers, *Sergeant Rutledge* (1960); Stanley Kramer's sermonic allegory,

15. Sidney Poitier's career spanned almost the entire postwar era. Poitier contended that as one of few black stars, he had a duty to portray only positive images, as in *The Lost Man.* (©Universal Studios)

The Defiant Ones. These films attracted black audiences, and their studios distributed advertising dollars accordingly; in return, they earned revenues from black neighborhoods.

Yet so little that could be called "black film" grew out of this period, perhaps because a rebirth of hope of eradicating past racial discrimination made uniquely black film statements counterproductive. One gem appeared: Michael Roemer's *Nothing But a Man,* a thin little film that caught the mood of rural black Alabama with such care and precision that one major urban library included it in its documentary collection, and James P. Murray, critic of the *Amsterdam News,* called it "the greatest of black motion pictures."

The situation changed drastically in the late 1960s. The period was marked not by a big cinema event but rather by a gradual shift of audience attention toward bolder, more political black films in keeping with a changing political climate abroad in the nation. Jones's *Dutchman* received keen attention from intellectuals, if not general audiences. Stanley Kramer's well-meaning *Guess Who's Coming to Dinner* was greeted by black laughter. Van Peebles's *Story of a Three Day Pass* (1968) attracted international attention. Radicals greeted *The Battle of Algiers* (1967) with strident cheers. And the TV news was filled with newsfilm of nationwide urban streetfighting. The age of the "blaxploitation" movie had begun, without forethought.

A new crop of films, among them *Shaft* (1970), adopted new modes and elements that played to a newly aroused audience. *Shaft,* the product of an interracial crew, but black-focussed advertising, was close enough to white heroic models to inspire "crossover" sequels, yet it deeply touched black urban youth with its specific references to their way of life. The hero, as played by Richard Roundtree, personified the outlaw whose streetwise skills served his society in symbiotic ways as a moralist-cop. *Shaft* was good for black movies. While it was typical of many black genre films, an *aesthetique du cool* gave it both identity and an advertising angle. Shaft's peculiarly black urban dress and flair freed him from the white heroic mode, thus recreating the detective-outlaw of *film noir* in black terms. Isaac Hayes's theme music, for which he earned an Oscar, sharpened the hero's identity.

Among other forms, *Sounder* and *The Learning Tree* (1968), which emerged from pastoral sources, were in the style of old fugitive slave narratives and spirituals that promised a land across Jordan. Both Martin Ritt and Gordon Parks, respectively, created pastoral genre films by combining a bucolic pictorial sense with a sure knowledge of their characters.

Even before Mark Twain's *Huck Finn* or the migration of the black folk legend, *Staggerlee,* to northern cities, Americans had

16. But for production problems and limited distribution that sapped its energy, Leroi Jones's (Imamu Baraka) *Dutchman* might have led a late 1960s movement toward a new black cinema. (Gene Persson; Nederlands Stichting Filmmuseum)

17. Pastoral films such as *Sounder* spoke to both black and white
("crossover") audiences through heroes who bore up under adversity
with quiet dignity. (© 20th Century-Fox)

18. The best films of the "blaxploitation" era were those like *Cotton Comes to Harlem* that were deeply rooted in a black ambience. (© United Artists)

enjoyed picaresque tales whose visionary heroes bobbed atop the currents of opportunity. This literary genre came to the black screen in the form of such films as Van Peebles's *Sweet Sweetback's Baadasssss Song* (1971), the film version of Faulkner's *The Reivers* (1969), and Raymond St. Jacques's *The Book of Numbers* (1972), each a spirited form of the familiar tale of the American trickster-hero.

So important was this subgenre to its audience that inferior attempts earned millions of dollars from black moviegoers in run-down urban theaters. Counterfeits of white films provided a neat black moral twist, a certain fresh absurdity, and another source of black films. Among them were *Cool Breeze* (*The Asphalt Jungle*) (1972), *Blacula* (*Dracula*) (1972), *Abby* (*The Exorcist*) (1975), and *The Lost Man* (*The Informer*). Others, like Chester Himes's *Cotton Comes to Harlem* (1970), were based on turbulent black novels. Even failures, either artistic or financial, like *Soul Soldier* (1972), *Honky* (1971), *Georgia, Georgia* (1972), *Black Jesus* (1971), *The Landlord* (1970), *Leo the Last* (1970), *The Angel Levine* (1970), and *The Bus is Coming* (1971) were not without interest, merit, or a sense of purpose.

Unfortunately, by the mid-1970s, the mood that had encouraged "blaxploitation" movies flagged before serious filmmakers took up neglected themes such as the familial centers of black life. Only a handful of these, like *Claudine* (1974) or *Five on the Black Hand Side* (1973), caught critical attention, and none earned outstanding profits. African subjects were rarely treated, and of these, only Ossie Davis's *Kongi's Harvest* (1971) came close to success. Except for the St. Claire Bourne-Woodie King poorly distributed feature, *The Long Night* (1976), no documentarist ventured into theatrical film. Black music on film never grew beyond compilations like *Wattstax* (1973) and *Soul to Soul* (1971), and Hollywood biographies such as *Lady Sings the Blues* (1972) and *Leadbelly* (1975). At the end of the cycle, then, few films of range and integrity stood out as alternatives to "blaxploitation" films.

The young black audiences who had originally supported "blaxploitation" films soon lost interest and shifted their allegiance to other genres including science fiction or martial arts films, which traded on violent revenge themes set in Oriental locales. Black youth, then, recoiled from fantasies of lust and power, choosing instead symbols from another culture that provided metaphors for Afro-American experience despite their Oriental settings. Martial arts films offered blacks comic strips of pure vengeance dramatized in a choreography of violence unobtainable within the literal context of American social realism. In an effort to recapture the youth market, black actors even began to imitate, without success, the film style of Run Run Shaw, Raymond Chow and other Asians.

By 1975 only foundation-supported and public television docu-

19. Herbert Danska (far left) sets up a shot for *Right On!* with actor-poets Gylan Kain, David Nelson, and Felipe Luciano (left to right). The film, a pastiche of cinema verité film, poetry, and improvisational theater, failed to inspire followers. (© Leacock-Pennebaker; courtesy, Herbert Danska)

mentarists broke from the pattern of exploitation. Carlton Moss, Madeleine Anderson, and St. Claire Bourne, whose credits included a rare interview film with Elijah Muhammad, were among the successful. Senior among them was William Greaves, who had worked in race movies, in Hollywood, for the National Film Board of Canada, and with television. Others, however, like Ben Land of Howard University, who made a film that was broadcast as a segment of NET's *Color Us Black* (1968), rarely worked at all.

After more than fifty years of a hot-and-cold history, black genre film, at least on theater screens, lapsed into stasis. Both apart from and dangerously close to Hollywood, black genre filmmakers remained fearful of usurpation, hopelessly dependent on funds from outside black circles, and therefore driven to seek wider audiences through so-called "crossover" movies. This, in turn, rendered them equally fearful of white condemnation, condescension, and over-praise. Nevertheless, black genre film has survived. The battle of a small racial minority to see its image and to define its identity on the screen has not been lost. Enduring, then, was a kind of victory.

Unfortunately, black genre film failed to penetrate the television medium, which in the last twenty-five years has gradually determined the format of motion pictures in America. Commercial television first attracted postwar audiences away from theaters, then began to make use of Hollywood's empty soundstages. Thereafter, film for theater distribution, in order to survive, reached for specialized audiences such as the "youth market" or "blaxploitation" fans, re-vived moribund genres such as horror films and science fiction, and larded their products with closeup violence and sex. At the same time more prestigious films explored social controversies, brought distinguished novels to the screen, or simply advanced the state of the art, attracting audiences in the face of the general decline. In contrast, the audience for television was an undifferentiated mass measured only by gross tabulations of audience samples expressed as "ratings."

Because ratings failed to reveal the size or tastes of the black audience, it was an easy matter to create television programs that avoided racial matters. Moreover, in commercial TV's long-estab-lished system of allocating frequencies to stations that based their profits on selling advertising time, an oligopoly of three networks has competed for a fixed audience. The result was a generation of conservative programming that depicted the broadest norms of American life. This tendency excluded references to Afro-American society as too precious or too deviant. Only a few local stations such as radio's WLIB in Harlem attempted to cultivate Negro audiences, and not until the 1950s did advertisers direct campaigns toward black broadcasters.

During World War II the liberal drift that had influenced movies also touched broadcasting. The Office of War Information urged the production of shows like Mutual's prime time *My People* (1943) and local programs like *Victory Through Brotherhood* (1943). Wartime dramatic programming joined the trend with such experiments as CBS's 1943 summer-replacement situation comedy, *Blueberry Hill,* featuring Hattie McDaniel, Mantan Moreland, and Savannah Churchill.

New York's stations led the way in local black broadcasting. WMCA's talk show, Roi Ottley's *New World A'Comin'* (1944) and its summer replacement, the Hall Johnson Choir, were followed by WNYC's song fest, *The Voice of the City* (1944) with Josh White. Despite a few old-fashioned shows such as the Blue Network's *Aunt Jemima,* the way seemed clear for a black penetration of broadcasting after the war.

Yet no one accurately predicted the impact of television on American life. Columnist Ed Sullivan promised that "television will not disturb the balance of show business," even as the makers of "soundies" made plans to dump more than one thousand of their titles on the TV market. The issue remained in doubt as late as 1949.

By 1950, the future of television became more clear, and with clarity came a more precise estimate of a possible black place in the medium. As early as July 1949, the *New Republic* predicted that, in view of TV's control by advertisers and the Federal Communications Commission, both of which were responsive to social pressures, the Negro should be able to open up television as a potent medium of black expression.

As if to test the prediction, the NAACP challenged CBS by setting out to drive from the air *Amos 'n' Andy,* a popular radio show that made its TV debut in 1950. For years Negroes winced at the show and yet enjoyed its broad satire of black life. But its coming to visible life on television was intolerable, no matter what changes sponsors, creators, or cast contrived. Eventually the NAACP campaign extended to sponsors, network, and press. The result was that the first black incursion into TV defined blacks negatively rather than as a developing black genre. Lost in the clatter was WOR-TV's *Harlem Detective* (1953), with classical actor William Marshall in the title role. Problems of sponsorship and blacklisting helped cancel the show without a murmur from black pressure groups.

The fate of *Harlem Detective* and *Amos 'n' Andy* became a model for the immediate future. Sponsors' timidity and political pressures combined to dampen the prospects for a black TV genre. Rod Serling's script about a Southern lynching was twisted into a relatively bland western. Sponsor pressure censored Josh White's singing of "The Free and Equal Blues." Sometimes, when advertising agencies did not intrude, southern stations themselves censored programs, among them ABC's "Close-Up" series film, *Walk in My Shoes* (1963), a sketch of black plight seen through a day in the life of a Harlem cabdriver.

The age of bland racial programs came to an end only as a result of the street fighting that gripped American cities from 1965–68. Network journalists brought strident images of black insurrection into American living rooms with, in the words of the NAACP's Clarence Mitchell, "a profoundly constructive effect." In the mind of one producer, television became "the chosen instrument of the black revolution." Indeed, the medium had greater impact with blacks than with whites. For many blacks, TV was their only source of information: more than one quarter of the nation's poor blacks watched television eight hours or more each day and black teenagers watched it five times as much as white teenagers.

Nevertheless, by mid-decade, *I Spy* was the only adventure show with a black lead, while CBS's *In Black America* (1967) series functioned with a lily-white staff. Other prime time series managed token integration—*Mod Squad, The Outcasts, Adam 12*—while Hal Kanter's *Julia* stood out as the only show with a single black star. *Variety* praised the trend as long overdue but still only a "multimedia stereotype." In later years the type would broaden to include black junkmen, teenagers, women, and petite bourgeoisie.

20. The television spy serial, *I Spy,* pioneered in bringing Bill Cosby's unthreatening and winsome persona to a "crossover" white audience. Here Cosby confers with Sheldon Leonard on a foreign location. (*I Spy* Production Records, Research Library, UCLA)

At last in 1976, *Roots* by Alex Haley inspired a TV version which promised to break the dull trend of black broadcasting. Yet the pressures of big-time publishing and TV helped to so alter the project that any well-read viewer would be dissatisfied with the result. Haley explained the pressures against developing a TV black genre from *Roots*: "Multi-million dollar book-publications and TV-production plans had been set irreversibly into motion, and there was finally no way to resist them any longer."

In other words, the black media event of the 1970s was rushed on the air, shaped by pressures outside its own integrity. The fact that it pulled an audience of 130 million became meaningless; its success merely pointed to the fact that there was no black TV genre. Certainly the actors did little afterwards. As Georg Stanford Brown (Tom the blacksmith) noted, "there just isn't anything of consequence to do." But David Wolper, producer of the series, found himself in an opposite situation. "I'm busier than ever trying to keep up with the response to *Roots*," he said. "And I'm starting on *Roots II*."

Even at the beginning, *Roots* as a TV project was stimulated more by the medium than by black concerns. In summer 1974, as the first fragments of Haley's book broke into magazines, Wolper Productions' Stan Margulis was searching for a rival to Universal's miniseries, *Rich Man, Poor Man* by Irwin Shaw. After Margulis and writer Bill Blinn (creator of *Starsky and Hutch*) began adapting the unpublished *Roots*, they moved further from Haley's story because they based their draft on Haley's methodology lectures, rather than on the story itself.

The evidence of *Roots*'s weighty impact is impressive. A.C. Nielsen's rating figures are widely quoted. Black travel agencies have initiated *Roots* tours. Pop-genealogy books abound. Public funds are allocated for "*Roots* projects." White ethnic groups have taken up the search for their own roots. Publishers and community colleges alike hustle to grind out study materials and audio-visual aids designed to revive black history courses. Public Broadcasting's

Black Journal interviewed Haley. And ABC is preparing not only sequels, but programs on the saga of Haley's research and motion pictures for possible theater distribution.

Notwithstanding the notion of *Roots* as a media event, its heady success, and its extended career in sequels and revivals, the series of films which described a black epic from Africa to Tennessee suggests caution with respect to an eventual black TV genre. Where closed circuit "guerrilla" television offers hope for future independent TV, for the moment the influence of advertisers, the vast sums that change hands in television deals, and the resulting urge to seek a "crossover" audience of millions hold out scant hope for the development of a black TV genre. As the history of motion pictures has shown, only small films made by committed filmmakers with finite resources have resulted in effective genre films. The experience of TV leads to the same conclusion: the smaller, uncelebrated public television programs allow for small-group control, which in turn results in viable genre offerings.

A Brief Analysis of
Six Black Genre Films

PART TWO

3   *The Scar of Shame*

Social drama has been the popular art form most often embraced by an audience at odds with its circumstances. As a vehicle for Afro-American sentiments, the social drama has allowed full range to the black film genre. Built on sensitivity to the black plight in America, narrowly focused on segregated circles, using the details of plot and incident as the basis of an anatomy of black social life, the social drama serves as the medium for expressing black aspiration. If the drama is set forth in an appropriate repertoire of symbols, the result conveys a strong sense of group consciousness. And in its optimistic forms, such as Lorraine Hansberry's *A Raisin in the Sun,* social drama can become almost a ritual of the eventual redemption of Afro-America.

The middle-class social drama has long been a staple of the American cinema. D.W. Griffith's earliest explorations from primitive film into edited narratives were neat little social dramas; *The Romance of a Jewess* (1908), for example, depicted familial conflict over the pain of assimilation brought on by a mixed marriage. In the most recent unfolding of television genres, social drama has grown into a new form that runs for entire evenings and even weeks. It should then be no surprise that a team of silent movie makers, black and white, should have turned the social drama into a subgenre of black film. Indeed, the work of the Colored Players in 1927 was not only in the tradition of social drama of middle-class life, but at the height of a resurgence of social themes in the silent cinema. It seemed the most natural mode for conveying the dense in-group point of view, the sense of urgent advocacy, the rich detail of good anatomy, the cool hero, the mythic rituals of aspiration and success, and the symbolic repertoire of black genre.

The Colored Players competed with a host of rivals, black and white, who saw similar possibilities. As early as the teens, the Ebony Motion Picture Company of Chicago and its black frontman, J. Luther Pollard, tried to reach an interracial audience by enlarging the inventory of black social roles. If their goal of universality proved false, it was not the fault of the medium; rather, filmmakers and producers were limited by their own narrow view that white audiences could tolerate only traditional Negro roles.

Toward the end of the silent era, a few Hollywood studios intended to make comedy out of anatomies of black society drawn from the stories of Hugh Wiley and Octavus Roy Cohen. Through the same period, black companies had similar goals, several of them adapting the novels and stories of Paul Laurence Dunbar, Charles Waddell Chesnutt, and even T.S. Stribling for the screen. Unfortunately, few of the resulting films survive. More than fifty years ago, for example, the Lincoln Motion Picture Company released *The Realization of a Negro's Ambition,* of which but a tiny fragment survives. Thus, we cannot study what may have been the earliest instance of a black success myth on film. Oscar Micheaux's *Body and Soul,* as we have noted, survives only in a form beset by censor-imposed ambiguities. Save for a fragment included in *Post-Newsweek's* television documentary, *Black Shadows on the Silver Screen* (1975), the movie remains inaccessible. Thus, the young, intense Paul Robeson's earliest, and in some ways, most complete genre film performance, the role that demonstrated aspects of social melodrama in the service of social criticism, is not available for analysis. Late in the 1920s another genre film, Richard D. Maurice's *Eleven P.M.* (ca. 1928), which survives in its entirety (although its origins remain a matter of discussion among historians) attempted to present a faithful visual record of Detroit's ghetto. But the authentic texture of the streetscape is soon discarded in favor of a curious, garbled reincarnation tale that seems foreign to its black theme.

No one has indisputably sorted out the clouded beginnings of the Colored Players, the most successful of these early groups. We know that in the mid-1920s, Sherman "Uncle Dud" Dudley, a veteran black vaudevillian, felt that Negro vaudeville was dying. We also know that a few white entrepreneurs, among them, Robert Levy (owner of the Reol studio where Dudley had made a race movie), were willing to invest in race films as a possible successor to black stage entertainment.

David Starkman, a white Philadelphian with a financial interest in movie theaters that were slowly turning to black clienteles began searching for films to schedule. Starkman offered to merge with Dudley, thereby opening the opportunity to create the "black Hollywood" in Philadelphia's Tempo Studio that Dudley had once dreamed of in Washington.

They first rummaged for an angle that would touch their black audience. The resulting film, *A Prince of His Race* (1926), now lost, taught the lesson that the black social ladder was both short and shaky, and those who reached the pinnacle might fall the farthest. In the same year, Charles Gilpin starred in their version of the old road show melodrama, *Ten Nights in a Bar Room,* a temperance tract to which Gilpin gave a double turn of the screw, because of his own reputation as a drinker, and because so many black migrants from Southern pietism feared that their people would fall victim to saloons, the demoralizing social forces pressing upon Northern black neighborhoods.

Then, together with the technical talents of Frank Perugini and Al Liguori, two white journeymen who directed and shot the film, Dudley and Starkman shared the social and technical knowledge that resulted in *The Scar of Shame.* Like many black creations in America, this film owed much of its substance to forces intruding from the white world.

The Scar of Shame, of all the black silent films, then provides the best example of the genre by virtue of its survival, its consistent point of view from within a black bourgeois subculture, its accurate anatomy of black social mores, its closely worked myth of black aspiration for "the finer things," and its arresting vocabulary of plausible supporting symbols.

This is not to say that *The Scar of Shame* was, as some of its advocates claimed, "a new standard of excellence," or the equal of Von Sternberg's early films, as another enthusiastic observer insisted. Nor was it, as a black critic observed, "possibly the finest product [of a] black-owned company" that therefore was somehow more "interested in true depictions of black culture." Instead of these artistic and political standards, *The Scar of Shame* took the measure of its rivals by virtue of its accomplishment as a genre film true to its point of view, segregated roots, narrative treatment of black aspiration, repertoire of black symbols, schematic anatomy of black life, and cool hero for whom style is more important than action. In short, by the end of the silent era, *The Scar of Shame* stood as the brightest spot in race movie making, measured by the specific standard of fidelity to a black genre, rather than by some purely aesthetic one.

"A child could have done it," is the way its star, Lucia Lynn Moses, recalled her role in the film. "They just told me what scene it was and we just acted it out," she said of her white bosses at the Philadelphia studio, to which she commuted from her chorus-line slot at the Cotton Club. Yet the film became more than the scheme of a handful of white exploiters to make a few dollars. The chemistry of black cast, white crew, and interracial production team created a remarkable document.

The Scar of Shame serves its theme so well that to isolate its parts for the sake of analysis begs the question of integrity to genre and audience. Its clearly sympathetic point of view, mythic quest for a better lot, careful use of contrasting symbols of power and poverty, and larding of melodrama with a detailed anatomy of the conflicting strata of black urban life, hold together the film as a strong exemplar of the genre. Out of these elements unfolds a theme rooted in the tension between street life and the black bourgeoisie. To rise above the one while avoiding the hypocrisy of the other should be the goal of the ambitious Negro. This, the message of *The Scar of Shame,* is asserted with firmer conviction than its intended sermon against color-caste snobbery. The message took on added sophistication because of the audience's familiarity with the reality of black life: the ghetto Negro who seeks the main chance brings to it a weighty burden of poverty, casual brutality, and the guilt that results from stepping over the fallen.

The film's dichotomy leaps from the screen from the first establishing shots. The flat gray world of the streets, with it hustlers and grifters, is set against the prim, neat rented room of a black composer. These symbols foreshadow the characters who will represent these opposites in a dramatic conflict. The composer, Alvin Hilliard (Harry Henderson), is dangerously close to betraying the less fortunate of the race. Through his mastery of white music that will carry him to a life of "the finer things," he is coolly escaping the ghetto. Outside his window are the darkened doorways and foreboding fenced backyards of black Philadelphia. The American success myth rules in his room; the urge to survive on the street. Hilliard's landlady expresses the middle-class code. He will become "the leading composer of our race," she predicts.

One day Hilliard, alone with his music, is drawn to the window by screams, which foreshadows a descent into the ghetto. In the yard below he sees Louise, a beautiful light-brown girl, being beaten by her brutal father. Plot and ambience quickly fuse. Hilliard, stiff in his neat clothes, clambers down the fire escape to the rescue. A short bitter scrap follows, and the loser is Louise's father, who, in contrast to Hilliard, wears a workingman's cloth cap and smokes his cigarettes down to ragged, pinched ends.

Louise and Hilliard enjoy a brief, chaste romance and plan a marriage of convenience that will rescue her from her father's rough discipline, and by implication, from the squalor of the ghetto. With each cutaway to life outside their neat cubicle—the gray exteriors, paper-strewn streets, and vacant, staring storefronts—the audience is reminded of the fate from which the marriage will save her. On the street, Eddie, a hustler and saloonkeeper, rules by a hard code. He leads Louise's brooding, drunken father into a plot to ruin her marriage and bring her back into his ghetto sphere.

These rivals for Louise's life struggle at the center of a black bourgeois myth of success. On the one hand the striving Hilliard and the passive Louise express an urge to escape the harsh life of the street. On the other, Eddie, knowing he cannot rise out of the ghetto, seeks to impose a Pax Negro upon it, to control that which he cannot escape. Here are the two sides of black ambition: the urge to flee the ghetto or to control it.

The filmmakers speak with conviction, an authentic black point of view, and a tragic sense by revealing the frailty of both black goals: escape cannot be complete nor dominance absolute. Eddie's hegemony extends only to those shattered by the ghetto experience. Hilliard's marriage to Louise is strained by his mother's furtive reluctance to accept the bride because she is "beneath our set."

These polar opposites of black life—middle-class aspiration and the life of the street, the "respectables" and the "riffraff," in the terms of historian David Gordon Nielson—are seen throughout the film in densely packed syntagmatic inventories of symbols that reinforce, illustrate, and allegorize the theme of conflict between the two sets of black social values. To cite only one example, Eddie contrives a ruse to draw Louise away from the security of her newly insular bourgeois life by diverting Hilliard to his mother's suburban home by a false emergency. The episode seems dramaturgically contrived and improbable; Eddie is too beastly and lacking in motive; Louise is too gullible; Hilliard's response is too mindless. But the visual statement is striking. The suburban houses are flat and stark; a similar though less powerful image than an Edward Hopper streetscape, they are as perversely empty of humanity as a child's Christmas-garden suburb. In contrast, Louise remains in

21. In *The Scar of Shame,* the room where Louise (Lucia Lynn Moses) dies symbolizes the life she relinquished by compromising. (© *Post Newsweek* Television)

the cluttered, vibrant city, in Eddie's hands. If this visual metaphor fails, it is only on the level of conveying the gradations of skin color that presumably form the basis for the Afro-American caste system. Lights and darks are muddled rather than divided into light bourgeoisie and dark proletariat, thereby giving greater weight to class striving symbols over those of color line. The dramatic conflict then is between those who seek "the finer things" and those who do not.

The rest of the plot unfolds out of the class conflict. The uneasy alliance between Hilliard and Louise eventually deteriorates; in a confrontation he wounds her and scars her neck, which she thereafter covers with a gossamer scarf. Hilliard is convicted, jailed, escapes, and becomes a piano teacher, while Louise begins a scarlet

career as a singer in Eddie's cabaret. Years later, Hilliard falls in
love with a pupil from his own class. When her roguish father has
a liaison with Louise, Hilliard and Louise meet. More proper than
ever, he refuses to be blackmailed into resuming their old relationship. Louise, realizing she is a "victim of caste," poisons herself,
allowing Hilliard to step over her corpse and marry into his own
class.

The cluster of visual symbols serves as an opening to an anatomy
of a black world, made necessary because black society, like American white society, is multi-faceted. As in many literary anatomies
from Izaak Walton's *The Compleat Angler* to Arthur Hailey's
Airport, the intention is to transmit information. But in recent times
the function of literary anatomy has enlarged to include melodramatic entertainment often cast in the mode of social drama. *The
Scar of Shame* was both good social drama and good anatomy in
this sense. In the form of a drama of manners it taught the audience
details of its own less-known lifestyle, challenged one of its value
systems, and illuminated the possible flaws in one black bourgeois
strategy in its struggle against racism. As a cautionary tale warning
Afro-Americans of the awful price to be paid by those who too
casually abandon the question of race solidarity, or who uncritically
adopt the white world's segregated system, *The Scar of Shame* derived a sense of conviction and power from the dense authenticity
of its social details and symbols. The black audience was reminded
sharply of what it already knew: moving to the suburbs, forsaking
urban roots, adopting white norms, cannot erase responsibility to
the darker brothers who can never escape.

If *The Scar of Shame* suffers from a theme which is not clear, it
is possibly the fault of title cards which informed the audience that
the film's dramatic tension was between light and dark. Recent
critics, too, have found it to be a cautionary tale about the evils of
color caste. But in fact, light skin appears in both high and low
castes, and the issue is more correctly one of aspiration. Every
single incident of plot and action depicts a question of upward

mobility. In the opening scenes in Hilliard's respectable boarding house, Eddie's bad manners spoil the decorum, and Hilliard literally drives him from the dining room. In another scene, Hilliard, who aspires to greatness as a composer, fights—and defeats—Louise's brutal lower-class father. In still another example, Louise's lower-class room is ironically dark and hopeless, while Hilliard's is brightened by a portrait of Frederick Douglass, the bourgeois black Republican hero.

Eventually it is Louise who symbolically abandons respectable black values. When she embraces Eddie's way of life, her childhood doll is crushed underfoot. "You too had to be a victim of caste," she says to her doll as she surrenders to life as it is and gives up the ideals Hilliard pursues. Moreover, Eddie sees the difference between their respective lives. He asks Louise to give up Hilliard for a life in his cabaret and calls Hilliard "that dicty sap." In 1927, "dicty" was the term used pejoratively to describe Negro social climbers, West Indians, and others whose manners set them apart from Negro folk style. As a final sign that Louise's decision to join Eddie spoiled her chance to aim for higher values, she becomes a shill in his cafe, itself corrupt because it masquerades in high-class style without the necessary substance. Hilliard, on the other hand, succeeds because his new life as a piano teacher is the result of solid "race ambition."

Hilliard and Louise continue to contrast: Hilliard offers Alice, one of his pupils, both love and aspiration; Louise is resigned to a dandy, who, in return for an introductory date, offers the news that he "hit the numbers today." Again, the point is hammered home. In contrast to Hilliard's substance and genuine ambition, the dandy offers the ephemeral goal of hitting the long shot in the gambling game played by the urban proletariat.

The iris-out ending of books and a candle symbolize, according to one character, a summation of Louise's wasted life. She failed to aspire for "the finer things," he says, not because of racism or color caste, but because she was a "child of her environment," and as such, failed to transcend squalor to embrace black bourgeois life. Hilliard, who aspires to success, lives, while Louise, whose vision never rises sufficiently to lift her above the low-life, must die.

But an ambiguity extends even to the sets, for much of the power of the last sequence springs from richly clustered symbols of class set in an ambience of cloying air, feather boas, antimacassars, and fringed tablecloths. These syntagmas signal both admiration and contempt, similar to that with which New York Negroes described Harlem's poshest street as "Striver's Row." On the one hand we see Hilliard rise through driving ambition. But on the other, we are reminded that although he personally avoids its consequences, his social climbing is anti-social, a desertion of the less fortunate of his race.

In conventional melodrama, Hilliard's course of action and its denouement would stand as a flaw in the plot because convention would not permit a romantic hero to be responsible for a death. But *The Scar of Shame* cannot be judged as an ordinary melodrama. The incidents of plot, setting, and character are dense with social meanings that provide visual signals through which a sensitive viewer perceives an anatomy of black social life and the social message beneath the contrived plot. That is, striving for the top of the black world has its price. On the way up, the striver may merely assimilate white tastes, as Hilliard seems to compose white music; but as Louise is scarred by the struggle, other blacks may be hurt by the individual's drive for success.

In *The Scar of Shame,* the surface indicators, the title cards, the apparent intentions of the filmmakers all pointed toward a conventional story about color caste. But the movie was transformed by visual imagery from a melodrama about caste into a film that turned in on itself, and discarded its surface message in favor of looking at the ambiguous lives of the dicty blacks on Striver's Row.

4 *The St. Louis Blues*

The early days of sound must be seen as a lost moment for black genre film. At last the motion picture became capable of recording the most ancient black mode of expression—folk music and dance. At the same time, Hollywood editorial controls were muddled by new technology, opening the opportunity for black intrusion into the Hollywood system. Indeed, during this brief, promising period, Bill Foster, one of the earliest black filmmakers, and Walter White, the soon-to-be Executive Secretary of the NAACP, shared a belief in a legend that on the first generation of sound recording equipment, black voices recorded with higher fidelity than white.

Unfortunately for Afro-Americans, Hollywood technical crews, augmented by a westward migration of Broadway voice coaches and theatrical directors, soon recovered both equilibrium and dominance over the medium of sound film. Nevertheless, in the pioneering years that coincided with the Great Depression, while sound technicians learned their craft, a few significant black musical movies surfaced. Characterized by a buoyant, flashing style, they pointed toward a future musical subgenre of black movies. Unfortunately for blacks, the early musicals adopted the short film format; as the rental structure for short films was a less precise measure of popularity than normal box office returns, the black genre filmmakers were thereby removed one step further from the audiences they desperately needed as sounding boards or feedback circuits. Nonetheless, black musical film survived as a subgenre until after World War II.

For its melding of the blues idiom with the demands of motion picture scoring and recording requirements, *The St. Louis Blues* was among the best of the genre. Because black music came to the screen less affected by white infusions, the film promised to emerge from the filmmaking process with unprecedented purity. W.C. Handy's original musical composition inspired the movie, and thus provided the basis for a successful blending of black music and filmmaking. Because the music itself came from deep within black social circles, it could provide aural reinforcement of segregated, inward-looking symbols of black life and enhance the meaning of the film. Thus if musical movies lacked generic traits—a sense of advocacy, an anatomical view of black life, and cool heroics—they transformed other traits of the genre into a rhythmic ritual which celebrated black life.

Black music had been changing in the twentieth century from a mainly rural tradition of shouts, hollers, and spirituals to a broader, less cohesive expression that included outrageous, jangling forms of more urban music: rousing funeral marches, ragtime, jazz, secular forms of blues, and intensely felt gospel songs. Good generic movies borrowed from both urban and rural traditions and a few managed to capture the spirited rivalry between the two modes. Like black heroes, twentieth-century black music embraced two common sources: the rich Southern rural folk tradition with its pastoral reverence, pride in survival, and covert political expression beneath the surface of the lyrics; and the equally densely packed urban tradition with its secular, more abrasive forms.

The two traditions spoke to the two black cultures only recently perceived as separate by historians. As Herbert Gutman has noted in *The Black Family in Slavery and Freedom* and John Blassingame in *The Slave Community,* rural Southern black society bore up so well under slavery that, contrary to Daniel P. Moynihan's view in *The Negro Family,* the black family did not suffer fragmentation until the rigors of the Great Depression shattered the family's economic and social foundations. For our purposes this means what music critics knew all along: that both traditions provide a rich musical heritage, and therefore, each contributes to black film music.

A few movies caught the conflict between the two spirits: the cohesive, rural, familial life of the South, and the contentious, fractious life of the Northern ghetto. Murray Roth's *Yamacraw,* Duke Ellington's *Symphony in Black,* King Vidor's *Hallelujah!,* Langston Hughes, Clarence Muse, and Bernard Vorhaus's memorable *Way Down South,* and even the latter day *Wattstax* succeeded in expressing the stresses brought on by the twentieth-century change from black pastoral to black urban life.

Among the standouts of the genre, Roth's *Yamacraw* defined the dilemma confronting Negroes on the verge of moving to the city from the rural South. Drawing upon James P. Johnson's music and Jimmy Mordecai's performance, Roth transformed the sentimental sources of Southern genre cinema into a black hymn to the agony of being caught between homesickness for the South and an itch to live in the urban North. *Yamacraw* opens on a cardboard silhouette of a Southern cabin, then tightens the focus onto old black parents who symbolize the enduring South. Part of the strength of the set derives from angular distortions reminiscent of the German expressionists. In front of the shack, two lovers clasp, wracked by indecision. Shadowed hands reach up in plaintive piety, forming what would become a visual cliché in later films. As the lovers walk down the hill, intercut with two-shots, a crane shot sweeps upward while Mordecai sings "Yamacraw;" as he hefts his bag on his shoulder, we know he will leave the farm. In contrast, the city is everything different: a symbolic montage of stark and jagged sets, a nappy-headed dancing girl, a noisy street scene, ending at last in the young black migrant's turning away and heading home southward. A trade paper called *Yamacraw* a "jazz symphony of Negro life that is arresting as well as dramatic." If the film lacked something, it was ambition. Running only a quarter of an hour, it grasped at the limited goal of contrasting urban with pastoral, and settled for small success.

Within months, two major studio productions, Vidor's *Hallelujah!* and Paul Sloane's *Hearts in Dixie,* attempted a similar theme by using the black musical idiom as a medium through which to record on film the Afro-American experience. In 1929, these two rivals for black audiences' attention wisely employed black counselors, Harold Garrison as an assistant director on *Hallelujah!* and Clarence Muse as star and adviser on *Hearts in Dixie.* Both of the films succeeded as sincere celebrations of black life and fortitude, even if they failed to be major hits of the genre.

Hallelujah!, for all its fidelity to Southern ambience, depended too much on Tin Pan Alley infusions of music rather than on black folk music. Unfortunately, when the plot moved to the city, Vidor's vision blurred and melodrama dominated over the anatomy of the black South with which he had opened the film. Despite touches of black piety, pastoral reverence, and stirring evangelism, the film lost its focus and surrendered to a busy, hard-working plot. *Hearts in Dixie* featured Stepin Fetchit's finest performance, a near-tragic role that slipped only slowly into his stylized comedy resented by so many middle-class Negroes. Its black religious ecstasy rang more hollow than that of *Hallelujah!* And its redemptive last sequence, a farewell to a child taking the steamer northward to study medicine in order to return to help his village, asked a lot of its audience's credulity. The achievement of *Hearts in Dixie* and *Hallelujah!* consisted more of their outreach to a surprisingly large white audience appreciative of some sort of faithful rendering of black folk life.

Duke Ellington's two films, *Black and Tan,* and especially *Symphony in Black,* represented the other side of an evolving black musical genre with an urban inspiration. Indeed, the films carried the medium a step further into the sound era by making highly integrated use of black music, and in the process, most certainly rivalled many major Hollywood productions. Ellington's films perhaps led the process of innovation precisely because they were black, short, and cheap, with no risk to either white money or white stars.

Each in its own way, *Black and Tan* and *Symphony in Black* combined eloquent black story lines, stylish, moody lighting and sets
that foreshadowed *film noir* of a later decade, and Ellington's music.
More than illustrated musicales, they were genuine genre films.

Symphony in Black, for example, rolled on the format of a symphony in four movements: the heavy cadence of the "middle passage" from Africa to the New World, the plodding grind of slave
labor, the jazzy beat of urbane Harlem, and the vaulting spirit of
black folk religion. A trifle too intellectualized, the film unfolded
in carefully structured order, but was more constrained by an urge
for correctness than for imagination. Throughout the four movements, the music changes texture and beat with each sequence of
dissolves that carries us through the forlorn halls of black history
but does not engage our spirits. The film comes alive in the Harlem
sequence because of a fleeting, erotic bit by Billie Holiday and Earl
"Snakehips" Tucker in a mottled streetscape. An upbeat evangelistic
sequence heightened the effects, and was partially responsible for
the rumor that the movie was in the running for an Oscar. If the
film seemed too much an exercise, it was not because Ellington was
merely a heartless craftsman, but rather, that in the early 1930s,
cutting filmed sequences to fit pre-scored music was still an unen-
viable task. *Black and Tan* took a narrative tack, allowing the music
to flow out of a thin story in which Fredi Washington, although
weak of heart, dances so Ellington can finish his "Black and Tan
Fantasy." She dies with its notes ringing in her ears, her deathbed
scene a darkened frame broken by Franz Kline strokes of black
on white.

Dozens of these little movies, none of them running more than
four reels, followed the example set by *The St. Louis Blues* and the
early Ellington films. They reached their most self-conscious artistic
apogee in 1944. Gjon Mili, a *Life* magazine still photographer, made
the brief *Jammin' the Blues* for Warner Brothers, an exercise that
was all lights, shadows, and cigarette smoke set to music. By abandoning the formal structure of the symphony, Mili allowed the tempo

of jazz to contribute to the cutting and pacing while shooting from varied angles which focused on a smoky jam session. But as Ernest Hemingway wrote of bullfighting, the precise moment of highest artistic refinement coincides with the first moment of decadence. Most musical shorts declined into two-camera setups featuring white bands that were performing near some under-used studio. A single black entrepreneur, Fritz Pollard, made "soundies," sixteen millimeter set pieces designed for marketing in visual jukeboxes, but he eventually sold out to white interests. By the late 1940s Billy Eckstine, a jazz singer who also reached for a popular audience, attempted to combine a jazz setting with a detective story in a style reminiscent of the then current *film noir*. But his *Rhythm in a Riff* (1947) failed to take off.

Not until *Wattstax* in the 1970s' post-insurrectionary years of black urban life did music open up to more cinematic treatment because of a willingness to shoot "quick and dirty" exterior footage using multiple camera setups in Los Angeles Coliseum's annual Watts festival. Ed Mosk's *Soul to Soul* (1971) also tried to enlarge the range of black musical film by intercutting from two sets of footage, one shot in West Africa featuring the Ike and Tina Turner revue, the other shot in Los Angeles with black African performers. But these outdoor pageants pointed toward the birth of a new genre apart from that introduced by *The St. Louis Blues*.

Dudley Murphy's *The St. Louis Blues* suffered more than the usual disabilities of independent genre film. Indeed *Variety* tried to reassure audiences that Afro-America was not accurately represented by the denizens of the saloons and circles of crapshooters who haunted the frames of Murphy's movie. If *The Scar of Shame* celebrated the black bourgeois hero's itch for success, *The St. Louis Blues* paid tribute to the hustler, an urban hero who won the game by exploiting its victims. Like Ruth Benedict in *Patterns of Culture,* early genre film sorted mankind into either straight, calculating Apollonian societies or volatile, mercurial, sensation-seeking Dionysian groups. The Colored Players shaped an Apollonian hero;

Murphy paid homage to the Dionysian sybarite. As genre film *The St. Louis Blues* rested on the strength of a segregated point of view and ambience, an anatomy of what Harlemites called the low life, and a cool celebration of black urban survival powers through Bessie Smith's blues singing, rather than via direct advocacy or heroics.

Murphy, at first glance, seemed an unlikely candidate to produce a black genre movie. A white man with raffish notions of Harlem life, a dabbler in avant-garde films, and director of a few Hollywood comedies, he held scant promise of making a sensitive black movie.

But lucky circumstances fell his way. Legions of black performers were at liberty as the Harlem Renaissance waned. New sound equipment and stages seemed to demand an idiom that would open new possibilities. W.C. Handy, the composer-arranger of blues, and J. Rosamond Johnson, author of the "Negro national anthem," the durable "Lift Every Voice and Sing," lent their music and talent. Legendary black performers were luckily free to work for a few days: Bessie Smith at the height of her powers, miniature comedian Edgar Connor, Isabel Washington, Fredi's sister, in a bit, and Jimmy Mordecai, the reed-slim, flashing dancer who made one of his rare film appearances.

Together they made the best black genre film of the early sound era. With slight pressure from the trade papers and censors, they could have created a smooth vehicle that would have been overpraised by white audiences, then forgotten. Instead, they gave free rein to Bessie Smith to display her hard-edged blues voice at its peak. Even a polished, harmonized chorus that intruded on the blues idiom upheld the spirit of the movie. The low budget and the New York studio conspired to add authenticity by denying the filmmakers the use of expensive and inappropriate stock shots and distracting locations.

By inadvertently limiting the inventory of images and symbols, the filmmakers gave the black contributors an increment of control over the product. These fortuitous circumstances worked to good effect in the film's opening. The script called for an establishing shot

22. Like W. C. Handy's original title song, *The St. Louis Blues* focused on the conflict between men and women over the issues of money and sex. The film starred Jimmy Mordecai and Bessie Smith.

of Beale Street, Memphis, that might have been a cue for a parade of flashy, street corner razor-toters; instead the release print opened on an appropriately dingy hallway.

Even then, the movie might have slipped into cliché, for the shot establishes the urban metier of the cocky hustler (Mordecai), who coolly outrolls the neighborhood's petty gamblers. Under the stairs we see a crapshooters' huddle, establishing the segregated circle into which we intrude. The players, rather than cookie-cutter stereotypes, are genuine characters, marked off from each other and rendered human by variations in bulk, style, and manner. The janitor's (and camera's) racial point of view and loyalties are communicated when he intrudes on the game and wheedles a cut of the action as payment for protection from "the white man [who] pays me to keep this place clean."

The game is merely a setup for Mordecai's entrance. Black audiences were already familiar with his reputation as a cool cat, and many placed his talent far above Bill Robinson's, whose success they attributed to his easy manner with whites. When Mordecai glides into the frame, he is like John Wayne playing a larger-than-life version of himself. A slim figure in a vested suit and homburg, he rolls the dice with a crooked smile, peeling off bets from a big wad of money. A pretty yeller woman ("you know they're liable to do anything," he says), the new girl in town, rolls the dice on her hip for luck and Jimmy scores, picks up his winnings, and leads her into his room.

So far, the shots are the conservatively chosen wide angles that cheap movies use as insurance against the risks of bungled experiments that require expensive retakes. But from the moment Bessie Smith enters, powerful, black, "looking evil," as she hears her name bandied by the circle of losers, she dominates, and the shots come closer. Eyes glaring, she walks right into the camera and out of the wide-shot under the stairwell. Scowling, her lip curling, she strides into Jimmy's room where he is explaining to his new "yeller gal" that they are not in Bessie's room: "she just pays for it."

As the new girl promises Jimmy a roadster, Bessie bursts in and roughs up her rival. She abuses the bluff janitor, then falls to the floor pleading with her man, promising him new suits. Lying at his feet, clinging, wheedling, she takes a sharp blow. In a last desperate gesture as he walks out, she takes a neat slug of gin. The shot comes in tight on Bessie. It is clear that Murphy intends her strong black presence to give character to the film even before she sings a note. Slumped half-upright on the floor, she begins crooning the classic blues theme, the loss of her man.

The cutting from one shot to another is often insignificant, but Murphy and his editor used cutting more effectively than had ever been done in the youthful medium of sound film. To get Bessie out of the dead-end binge on the floor, the camera comes in tight. Then a slow fade to black takes us out of the shot into a fade up on her down-turned, mournful face; she keeps singing without missing a note. Pulling back, we see and hear her perfectly synched song, but now she is leaning on a bar, nursing a mug of beer.

With Smith's voice over the scene, the camera flows over the large room peopled, one imagines, by friends at a party. Waiters glide by, spinning trays in fleeting closeup; a stiffly posed band plays Handy's music as the camera pans; at the tables, ringsiders harmonize a chorus backup to Bessie. At last the camera settles on a louvered door, raised above the crowded floor.

Through it comes Jimmy Mordecai, cool and sleek. Everyone knows him, and he greets them with a tip of his homburg, receiving their homage with a grin and a few bars of a dance. The camera comes in tight, the cuts flashing from his blurred feet back and forth to his fluid body. The camera barely follows the blinding tempo. The viewer, black or white, has intruded on an arcane world.

Jimmy ends with a low bow near the downhearted Bessie and greets her with exaggerated but hollow ecstasy. They dance in grinding slow time with the music, an erotic bit that *Variety* explained away as a trait, not of Negroes, but of the demi-monde, somewhat like the apaches of Paris. Bessie brightens at the apparently easy reunion, which lasts until Jimmy filches the money in the top of her stocking and triumphantly struts through the door.

The film ends by again narrowing our attention to a tight profile closeup of Bessie Smith at the bar. Supported by the chorus, she takes up her blue refrain. The whole sequence becomes a smokey blue visual symbol of the meaning of the blues, while it avoids stereotyping the black deviants from the straight black bourgeois milieu.

Throughout the film the small Gramercy Studio where it was shot allowed a fine control over the textured lighting and the pleasingly claustrophobic setting, thereby heightening the feelings of insularity, in-group tension and rivalry, and the intrasexual competition for scarce dollars. The orchestrated and arranged music suggested, without overpowering, the mournful idiom of the real blues. Together the music and the setting put the black demi-monde into ritual form that depicted black life without the need for formal elements of anatomy and advocacy. Mordecai's cool jazz dancing and Smith's blues singing were so pointedly on target that any more literal attempt to render black life would seemed didactic.

If it had a weak spot at all, *The St. Louis Blues* suffered the limitations imposed by using stars from other media. Like athletes whose fame is exploited by the movies, Bessie Smith and Jimmy Mordecai could be asked to reach only uneven middle levels of conviction even if, like Gary Cooper, they attempted only to play themselves. And it was certainly true that their characters seemed closely modeled on their actual personae. Therefore, no matter how well the movie succeeded in reaching its ambition, its brevity and inexperienced cast allowed it to attain only the small success of doing a small thing well.

5   *The Blood of Jesus*

Religious themes and their variants constitute the most self-contained subgenre of black film. And yet the large number that have appeared preclude the forming of sharp-edged categories. At its most inspirational, religion speaks through myth, ritual, symbol, and in-group advocacy. By defining rules of conduct, it provides its celebrants with a personal anatomy of the good life. At the other end of the scale of variants, religious film has been overintellectualized, sermonizing, falsely pious, literal, barren of pregnant symbols, and capable of serving only to half conceal that which the faithful were supposed to excoriate. Like Cecil B. DeMille's biblical epics which titillated the audience with moral ambiguities, black religious genre films always ended properly with a punitively apocalyptic last reel.

Often Hollywood religious movies suffered from timidity cultivated by the practice of soliciting theological opinions from clergymen or by making flatteringly unctuous portraits of popular divines such as Norman Vincent Peale. As an example, DeMille regularly called upon the influential Jesuit, Father Daniel Lord, for counsel on the technical theological details that went into the manufacture of his great crimson movies. The result was harmless colorful pap that snaked between watchful Jews on the alert for anti-Semitism dressed in bible stories and the Catholics' Legion of Decency and other watchdog agencies looking for presumed blasphemies. As a result, ethnic traits all but disappeared from Jewish depictions, and Catholics were shown as dynamic football coaches, *Fighting Father Dunne, The Hoodlum Priest,* and the whimsical elfin priests of *Going My Way.* Protestants, lacking such institutionalized scouts and friends at court, fared less well and appeared only in stodgy pieties such as the biography of religious pop culture heroes like Peter Marshall in *A Man Called Peter.*

In a rare, if accidental, position of strength, black filmmakers were freed from such constraints because their specialized audience preferred more direct religiosity. Indeed, because a few black filmmakers worked as genuine primitive artists, their own lack of expertise contributed innocently to powerful statements of faith and meaning quite beyond the Hollywood-produced films. Unfortunately, small homogeneous audiences composed of the faithful few hardly encouraged wide and prosperous distribution.

Thus of all the black subgenres, the religious tracts seemed most in danger of falling into parochial channels of meaning. In the 1930s, for example, Eloise Gist used highly personal films depicting literal symbols of her fundamentalist faith. For her, the act of sin invoked the real threat of devils, who carried sinners as passengers on an actual train to Hell. Because the images were intended to serve a flock of true believers, Gist felt no duty to aesthetics. Therefore her power resided only in her conviction and touched only the members of her cult.

Coincident with Gist's creative years, King Vidor's treatment of black religion was almost too persuasive and therefore implausible in its ability to evoke an immediate conversion experience. In *Hallelujah!* the rebirth of an amoral saloon girl, Chick, often brings an uncomfortable laugh. No matter how effective are his dramatized sermonic allegories, Zeke, a preacher, converts her so rapidly that she is merely out of character.

Later religious film attained greater political and social sophistication. Among the best modern examples was St. Claire Bourne's *Let the Church Say Amen* (1973), a straightforward television documentary whose spirit was touched more by cinematic training than by religious conviction or lifelong observation of Southern lore. Its strength was in its advocacy rather than its liturgy—specifically in a plea for a reexamination of the black church's apparent conservatism during the civil rights movement. Unlike other films on black religion, St. Claire Bourne's folk religionists were thus spoken for by an outsider employing an intellectual approach and craftsmanship.

This is not to say that all the subgenre films took the form of political or religious tracts. Gordon Hitchens's and Ken Resnick's *Sunday on the River* (1961), an alternately moody and spirited visual poem, broke out of the rigid mold of social realism that most American documentary had inherited from the age of *The March of Time* and Robert Flaherty. By using, rather than merely recording, visual reality, the filmmakers focused on the details of social anatomy as symbols in a sometimes unconscious allegory whose point of departure was a Sunday excursion down a Harlem street, to a Hudson pier, and then up the river to Bear Mountain Park. A track of lilting folk music accented the visual imagery of a pilgrimage from streetscape to green space. The technique impressed film critics and juries at Venice, Melbourne, and other international film festivals.

The neutral and quiet treatment of *Sunday on the River* stood in contrast to several others based on harsh anatomical reportage that laid bare black religion. For example, in his Rockefeller Foundation-supported *Black Delta Religion* (1975) released by the Center for Southern Folklore, William R. Ferris, Jr. followed King Vidor's lead in taking an anthropological point of view. This little film, a blow up from super-8, recorded the fervor of a black flock, its cadenced preacher, its women "getting happy," a baptism in a Southern river, and ended with a symphony of clapping, guitars, and tambourines. Reportage predominated over symbolism.

In contrast, *Sunday on the River* was a tour de force of symbol, metaphor, and allegory presented at the expense of literal anatomical details and the rhetoric of advocacy. The film opens on a sunny

Harlem street that cannot hide the squalor of broken buildings and rubble-strewn lots. A flurry of cuts moves the viewer from old folks lounging on the steps and curbs to sleekly proud kids, sometimes capped by a processed forelock, in Sunday best. These are symbols of survival and urban energy. The theme is affirmed as wise ancients stolidly watch a parade of youthful, uniformed, strutting churchgoers enroute to the pier where they will embark for Bear Mountain, a formerly lush resort fallen on hard times and now surviving on black church picnics.

By now the Hudson has become the Jordan. The music, off and on, sings of redemption, peace, and marching out of Egypt: "Ain't Gonna Study War No More," "I'm Crossing Over Jordan," "Children, Go Where I Send Thee," "Fare Thee Well," and "Hush Storm." We are not merely leaving Harlem; we are abandoning secular cares for an idyllic interlude in the heaven of Christian salvation.

Once on board, Ken Resnick's camera is lulled by the lazy rhythms. Kids dance, oldsters sit and take in the scene, lovers touch lightly. Slowly the controlling (and unconscious) metaphor takes over as the steamer slides under the George Washington Bridge. The sweep and curve of the towers and cables form a parabolic metaphor for the crossing into the promised land, an image that sits like a cat in the back of one's mind, stroked by the song on the sound track. At the instant of creation, the symbol meant little. A blurb-writer for the film said merely that they "cast aside their daily cares to have a good time." The cameraman shot the bridge only as a signal that the ship was under way, but to a recent black audience it was a parable in modern idiom. The ship's innards share in the visual allegory. The pistons, oiled and machined smooth, seem an engine of God driving the chosen people to a new Canaan.

The image is confirmed at Bear Mountain when the old boat sidles up to the ancient and rotting pier. The flock frolics, picnics, and lounges on the grass slopes rolling up from the river. Only the theology seems flawed, for as the outing comes to an end, we know they are not in paradise, but only a respite from the city, a shared and fleeting prophecy of a heaven deferred. They return home to Harlem. Like many allegories, *Sunday on the River* does not fit in all its parts, but its intimations of a special black paradise promised and withdrawn remains a powerful, unifying image.

Spencer Williams's *The Blood of Jesus* (1941) lacks Eloise Gist's totally naive faith, St. Claire Bourne's intellectual rigor, and Gordon Hitchens's and Ken Resnick's poetic flair. It does not rest on a hidden allegorical system or objective reportage. It is all surfaces, melodrama and fundamentalist lore, and the viewer can see the stitching at its seams. But it is the best extant example of primitive black religious film unadorned by artifice. In place of the intellectuals' symbolic cosmology the audience sees the black-and-white, good-and-evil, yang-and-yin of Southern black Baptist tradition rendered in melodramatic form on grainy film.

Williams, a great round, brown-skinned man, who hid a humorous streak behind his penetrating eyes, came to Hollywood in the late 1920s after a stint in the Army. He worked in Al Christie comedies as a writer and actor, and appeared in at least one race movie. After a lull during the Depression years, he caught on with Jed Buell and other makers of black westerns (one of which made *Time*'s movie section), and appeared in "B" movies and exploitation movies such as Richard Kahn's *Son of Ingagi*. His access to the screen closed only after Ted Toddy's Atlanta-based Dixie National Pictures bought up, standardized, and controlled the flow of race movies.

Sometime in 1940, a fellow Texan, Alfred Sack, asked him to make a few race movies to fill the product shortage brought on by Toddy's oligopoly. One result was *The Blood of Jesus,* an evangelistic tract in the style of Eloise Gist, but with a melodramatic sense sharpened by Williams's years in Hollywood. Indeed, Williams's achievement may have approximated Gist's goals. Although lacking access to Hollywood's technical crafts, Williams was able to adapt primitive, naive style to melodramatic formula in a way that appealed to both Gist's church-hall audience and the theatrical trade.

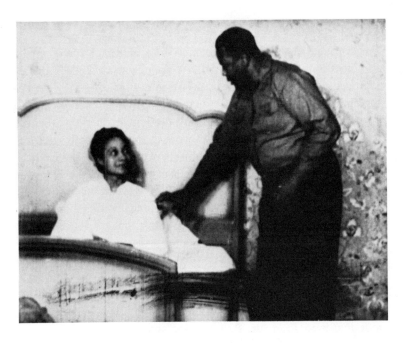

23. Spencer Williams (right) wrote, directed, and starred in *The Blood of Jesus*. (Courtesy Ken Jacobs)

Sack's brother and co-worker remembered it as the most durable and profitable race movie ever made.

Williams not only directed *The Blood of Jesus* but wrote the script and appeared in it as well, along with a crew of well-intentioned black Texas amateurs leavened by Reverend R. L. Robinson's Heavenly Choir. The result was an exemplar of Southern black fundamentalism untrammeled by white intrusion—even by Sack, who provided only money and distribution.

Like a series of Sunday School posters, every image and symbol assumed literal and larger-than-life fundamentalist proportions in a cautionary tale warning the faithful against the sinful life. Upright, decent, bourgeois blacks literally take up the struggle against the forces of the devil. But they are not the heroic masses of a

Sergei Eisenstein film; they are more like Hezdrel's forces in the forgotten militant sequences of *The Green Pastures*. Indeed the inner turmoil of the heroes of virtue is seen not collectively in sweeping shots of masses, but in a manner much like that of Slavko Vorkapich: slow dissolves and multiple images that reveal inner struggles with self. Thus Williams's work sprung from Hollywood tradition. Yet both his remoteness from the white studios and his tight budgets overawed Hollywood style and grounded *The Blood of Jesus* firmly in uncompromising sources of black Southern piety.

The film opens on a great cross in the clouds which is underlined by traditional black music. An old-fashioned iris carries the eye to a black farmer, then in closer and tighter to rough hands on the plow handles. Like the long crane shot that opens Orson Welles's *Touch of Evil*, it tells the viewer almost more than he is entitled to know at this early point in the film. But it is a neat device for putting the viewer's eye into the segregated world and for foreshadowing the religious tone that is to dominate. Pulling back, the camera takes in a wide shade tree with two blacks seated under its branches. At last a voice-over explains why we are here.

We intrude on this scene in order to mourn the passing of the great days when Afro-Americans were embraced by a familial certitude that would be later shattered by the great black diaspora from Southern farm to Yankee city. "Those days are almost gone," the voice says. "Almost. . . . " In this way we learn that somewhere in the South, a deeply rooted filiopietistic black morality survives as in a down-home Zion held out to urban blacks whose city life has failed them. Not until Gordon Parks's *The Learning Tree* a quarter of a century later, would a black filmmaker pay such homage to traditional life. Perhaps the urgent, immediate, urbane images of *aesthetique du cool* that so readily lent themselves to "blaxploitation" were responsible for diverting black attention away from the richness of rural tradition.

Although the viewer does not yet know why, the camera picks up a long queue of singers in Sunday best walking along a dusty road.

24. In *The Blood of Jesus,* an early sequence establishes the religious theme in a series of primitive but remarkably composed figures and spaces, lights and darks, and angular planes formed by a river baptism. (Courtesy, Ken Jacobs)

As we hear "All God's Chillun" and "Amazing Grace" on the sound track, at last we learn that they march toward their baptism in the broad reach of a river. Camera work is poor and lighting unmatched, but the imagery, except for a few evangelical sequences in *Hallelu-jah!,* is unlike that in any other American movie. It is a genuinely personal vision of faith untrammeled by art or skill—a true primitive sequence in the art critic's sense of the term.

Coming in tightly, almost as though the camera is standing in the water that has been stirred to muddy opaqueness, we see a pretty young woman receive her baptism with exceptional calm. Cutting away to a pair of gossips, we learn that she is Sister Jackson, new wife to Ras Jackson, who is hunting instead of attending the baptism. In a fleeting cut that foreshadows trouble, we see Ras running from a snake across a dry wash. Once home he admits that his hunt has been not for wild game but a sack full of shoats he has stolen to fill the empty larder. The audience may sense that the snake is an omen of bad tidings, for what good can come to a man stealing on the day of his wife's baptism? In the Jackson's cabin, the young wife pleads without success for Ras to get religion. Drained by the effort, she crawls into bed, under a *kitsch* Jesus on the wall.

The expected trouble follows shortly. Ras has leaned his shotgun against a chair and it falls of its own weight, firing a blast into his wife's room, striking her. Ras rushes in, sobbing.

The flock hovers over the dying Sister Jackson, with intercuts to Ras which show his remorse as he holds his head in his hands. The sequence becomes a flurry of cuts, from the bed, to the wide-eyed, wounded woman, to the humming flock dressed in white, to the spirit world and the pearly gates where the struggle for a soul will commence. "Swing Low, Sweet Chariot" resounds on the sound track as Ras falls, sobbing, to the bed. The saddened flock joins him, first chanting in unison, then in scattered personal pleas for the Sister's salvation. A voiceover sings "Give Me That Old Time Religion." Ras himself begins to sing and looks to heaven. But it is too late. One of the sisters draws the covers over the still form.

From this point in the film, the secular world shares the audience's attention with the world of the spirits. With Sister Jackson apparently dead, we fade out on a series of stylized religious tableaux: a trail winding heavenward, the portrait of Jesus on the wall, the gates of paradise, a shadowy but literal Jacob's ladder, a long-tressed angel superimposed over the bed, lifting the shroud. "This is the end of the trail," a voiceover says as wraiths and spirits lead Sister Jackson to her reward.

Not only have we been lifted out of the constraints of modern skepticism, but Sister Jackson's death becomes the occasion for a recapitulation of the history of her race. Ghostly monuments are built as the race moves forward. The combination of fundamentalism and racial history takes on the texture of a Cecil B. DeMille epic done on a shoestring.

Returning to the secular world, Williams makes Sister Jackson's soul the prize in a struggle between good and evil. As a test, her ghostly figure is again given substance and she is led down the path to temptation, past the false prophets and hypocrites. Each painterly scene provides a testament to the literal presence of God in combat with Satan. Indeed, Satan appears, garbed appropriately in white, and sends a flashily dressed Judas Green after the woman. "Go ahead Judas, do yo' stuff," he commands. And Judas tempts her with stylish clothes.

"You'll need them in the city," he says, and thus we know that the good rural life stands in sharp contrast with urban decadence. Judas and Sister Jackson go to a saloon, watch a few musical routines, and listen to a driving little band "beat out a little jive." Judas, along with a comrade, plots a wicked course for Sister Jackson, promising to "put [her] to work right away" in a life of sin.

Sister Jackson cries out for mercy and flees, first through darkened doorways, then into open country. Out there, near the good life, the odds shift in her favor. Nearby, a jazz piano plays on the back of a truck in a last tempting gesture, and two hand-painted signs point to either Hell or Zion. The audience knows Sister Jackson is saved when she crawls across the rough land to a cross as the voices of a choir rise in song. Blood drips from the crucifix above as a cut takes us back to her deathbed where we, and the mournful Ras, see her revive. The flock breaks into a hymn praising the miracle of her redemption. The audience can guess that Ras, too, will join the heavenly throng in gratitude for his wife's revivification.

Williams larded the film's ambience with a number of devices that lent textural support to his theme. In order to reinforce the conflict between city and country, for example, he cast the Devil in the style of *aesthetique du cool,* i.e., as the smooth and oily trickster, the natural enemy of pious country folk. Judas, his messenger, dresses

25. In *The Blood of Jesus,* the literal resurrection of Sister Jackson (Cathryn Caviness) from her deathbed results from the prayers of the flock, who stand under the benign portrait of Jesus. (Courtesy Ken Jacobs)

in flashy, cool clothes topped by a rakish fedora and glides with the cool stride of the street hustler—the bête noir of the black bourgeoisie. Like the secular counter-bourgeois images of *The Green Pastures* that symbolized urban evil, the heavies in Williams's film also haunt saloons crowded with finger-popping jitterbugs, dancers who embrace too closely, and even a woman in white picking a pocket.

All of the crowded images lead to a single unspoken point. As in black Southern folklore (reaching back to the days when Booker T. Washington founded Tuskegee Institute, and in his Sunday evening talks warned his pupils against going to town on Saturday), rural

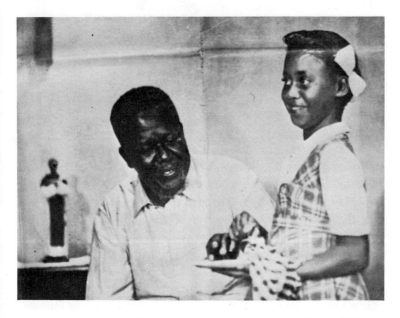

26. Like *The Blood of Jesus,* Williams's *Brother Martin* featured him as a primitivist-director and actor.

piety is pitted against urban disingenuousness. For decades, even in slave times, black preachers and teachers had warned their people away from cities. The movie concurs and tries to show that in town, the Devil drives.

To satisfy those with a faith in a more mechanistic god, the experience of Sister Jackson's miraculous recovery may be taken as a dream that she has shared with the audience. Here Williams performed his own miracle. While wearing his fundamentalism on his sleeve, he also allowed the disbelievers in the audience to accept the story because they can believe that the shot passed cleanly through Sister Jackson. However, this interpretation does not spoil the movie for the devout; for them, it is the true blood of Jesus that drips from the crucifix and the portrait on the wall, thereby symbolizing the power of God to intervene in the earthly affairs of the faithful. Thus last minute rationalism did not deny them their parable.

Such visual evidence suggests that Williams was more than a low-budget DeMille. He reached not for DeMille's audience, or for that of northern race movie makers. He aimed for Eloise Gist's audience in order to draw them out of their southern black church basements into theaters. Williams's religious movies were, for these audiences, simple, direct, and literal with symbols that carried their messages on the surface.

Williams completed the film just before the outbreak of World War II. During the war, a shortage of raw film stock curtailed the production of race movies, thus preventing Williams and Sack from making a sequel. Nevertheless, Williams managed to turn out *Marching On,* a tribute to black soldiers in the form of an adventure film in which black GI's expose a Japanese spy ring.

But toward the end of the war, Williams returned to religious themes for, as his backer claimed of *The Blood of Jesus,* it "was possibly the most successful of all the Negro films and lived the longest. . . . and possessed that certain chemistry required by the Negro box office." In 1944 Alfred Sack released Williams's *Go Down Death* which was "reverently" dedicated to the Afro-American poet James Weldon Johnson, whose poem had inspired the title.

Unfortunately, Williams never recovered the unique formula which he achieved with *The Blood of Jesus.* The times themselves may have altered the audience. Already on the move out of the rural South, black emigrants were further stimulated by the overheated northern industrial wartime economy. The very primitiveness of Williams's style and imagery was lost on a more urbane audience with access to Hollywood theatrical motion pictures. For years southern black fundamentalists had eschewed commercial movies in favor of films like *The Blood of Jesus.* Wartime changes in social values loosened their grip on their flocks and their tastes in entertainment. Williams, a born Southerner and a prodigal who returned home to Texas, was probably the last filmmaker to have an audience who could appreciate movies infused with sincere old-fashioned southern piety. Postwar audiences expected more art. To Williams's audiences drawn from old church basements, the fact that his work did not achieve artistic success did not diminish the power of his religious message.

Putting aside such questions of aesthetics and viewing the film only from the point of view of Williams's rural southern audiences, *The Blood of Jesus* stands as a remarkable if curious genre film. Like any genre film, *The Blood of Jesus* succeeded in the eyes of its fans even as its detractors scoffed at its lack of artistic pretension or its deviation from even the simplest canons of cinema art. As a genre film *The Blood of Jesus* emerged from segregated sources and perspectives. It provided a brief anatomy of Southern Baptist folk theology by presenting Christian myth in literal terms that pious fundamentalists could accept. From its opening voiceover, the film became an advocate for the most enduring traditions of Afro-American family life on southern ground. And it succeeded in characterizing the Satanic forces in black counter-bourgeois terms easily understood by the prospective audience—the "bad nigger" of the streets styled in the grand manner of *aesthetique du cool.* It worked as genre film, if not art.

6 *The Negro Soldier*

It cannot be said that there is a clearly black mode or style in documentary film. Over the years, theatrical and television documentaries, and educational and classroom films have reported or depicted various elements of black life and history. Some, especially the more reportorial, were not only made by whites, but were intended for the instruction of white audiences. In treating documentary film, the defining criteria for black genre become blurred, or worse, serve as a procrustean bed by which the films are shaped to fit artificially designed categories. The reasons for this critical problem are clear. Films about American racial arrangements consider the common themes of segregation, caste, anatomies of black life, and use an appropriate set of visual symbols that permit the filmmaker to deal with racial matters.

Even if we isolate some broad trait, such as a radical point of view, the outlines of black documentary genre remain muddled. The advocacy of some fashionable black political issue, for example, would allow us to categorize a black film as "black" only so long as the issue remained popular. Thus in the case of documentary, the traits of black genre film may be used only as an aid to understanding, rather than as a means of establishing positive identification.

We only know what seems unblack. William C. Jersey's arresting *A Time for Burning* (1966), a film made for the largely white Lutheran Film Associates, attracted little attention among black audiences and reviewers. All of the commentators who wrote advertising blurbs were white. The film purported to deal with the gradual integration of William Youngdahl's Augustana Lutheran Church in a formerly lily-white neighborhood in Omaha. After viewing an equally probing follow-up, *A Time for Building* (1967), one reviewer felt that "a few more black" participants would have provided better balance. The visual reporting of white agony and resolution of white problems simply lacked interest for black audiences, except as evidence of white failings.

On the other hand, good films made by both blacks and white can be rooted in the tastes and techniques of either race. Certainly the previously discussed *Sunday on the River* by white filmmakers Ken Resnick and Gordon Hitchens, which evoked a touching, lyrical black church outing, does not lend itself to a precise labeling of its makers' racial identities. An equally fine film, St. Claire Bourne's *Let the Church Say Amen,* used every standard device of white filmmaking so that it muted any traits that might expose a racial identity. Bourne's urbane, northern sensitivity to a black southern church imparted the same thrill of discovery that might have inspired an anthropologist's film of a pristine tribe. Bourne, for this reason, gave the film the careful reportorial tone imposed by the outsider's eye.

In another film Bourne clearly scooped the entire corps of American filmmakers with his exclusive interview with Elijah Muhammed, the leader of the American Black Muslim movement. The intellectual fashion of the time dictated that if so required by black leaders, black and white centers of life were to remain separate. Thus, the film, which was shot according to the then current techniques of shooting "talking heads," was black chiefly in the sense that its subject, Elijah Muhammed, knew Bourne was black and therefore, found it ideologically possible to grant him an exclusive audience.

Another social documentary filmmaker, William Greaves, built a durable career on reportage and liberal sentiments. Of all the black filmmakers, he alone soaked up experiences that carried him into a broad stream of work that defied parochial limits. Beginning his career in race movies just after World War II, he won a role in the pioneering message movie, Louis DeRochemont's and Alfred Werker's *Lost Boundaries* (1949), then migrated to Canada in search of production experience where he became a pupil and colleague of Norman McLaren at the National Film Board of Canada. He has produced both compilation and photo-documentaries of uncommon merit.

Greaves's two most famous works, *Still a Brother: Inside the Negro Middle Class* (1968) and *From These Roots* (1975), illustrate the norms of style and subject that mark black documentary, while at the same time giving it an identity similar to that of white filmmakers. Many documentary filmmakers, like other liberal Americans, believe that liberal change is possible and to be hoped for, and feel that powerful interest groups are subject to influence, even defeat, by coalitions of minorities, youth, urbanites, organized labor, etc. If they do entertain hopes for revolution, they just as often fear to lose what has already been gained.

In this liberal sense, Greaves has been the classic Afro-American filmmaker for whom artful film advocacy of a black cause has led to success. His work is an indication that good, tough-minded advocacy film does not lead to black nationalist revolution, but to lucrative bookings, production grants, television contracts, and more good movies. This fact helps make black and white film indistinguishably congruent, at least in their political rhetoric, if not their style.

If anything identifies black genre documentary film, other than perhaps accessibility to locations and subjects, it would be urgency of advocacy. Greaves's *Still a Brother* managed to emerge as a good anatomy of the black middle class. But the film's caste mark was its insistence that, despite the trappings of status and affluence described in E. Franklin Frazier's harsh polemic, *Black Bourgeoisie,* financially successful and well-placed blacks remained in the forefront of the civil rights movement. The effect was to pull one's punches, in keeping with the ancient commandment of the slave quarter, that no black man criticize a brother in the presence of the master class. With sometimes biting satire but overall evenhandedness, Greaves allowed the black bourgeoisie to indict itself, while pleading for a modicum of sympathy for their well-heeled plight as marginal men astride two cultures. With sensitivity his anatomy revealed the pretension and self-serving of the black middle class while verbally crediting the group with a social consciousness challenged by the preening images on the screen.

Greaves's *From These Roots* stood equally prominent as the finest film ever produced on the history of the Harlem Renaissance of the 1920s, and a tour de force that demonstrated the possibilities of the compilation technique for black subjects. But it also revealed that the same archival resources were available to whites, who might use them to construct similar segregated points of view, detailed anatomies of time and place, and a symbolic system that recreated the Harlem Renaissance as a mythic triumph of achievement over adversity. This fact of life, this accessibility of visual sources, meant that in documentary, talent mattered more than race. Greaves's work affected audiences because he was good, not because he was black. The same principle held for Bourne, television producers Madeleine Anderson and Tony Brown, and the generation of new black filmmakers.

Even advocacy fails as litmus paper. Ely Landau's documentary of *Martin Luther King* (1970) combined a fine journalistic sense, a dogged pursuit of forgotten footage, a sweeping, effective marketing device, and the urgency of a fund raising campaign for the Martin Luther King Foundation. Like a once-in-a-lifetime farewell tour of Jenny Lind, Landau sold it in a nationwide, supposedly one-shot saturation booking, after which the film was rereleased in sixteen millimeter format so as to earn, as Landau said, "continuing revenues from schools, colleges, churches and the like" for the future use of the Foundation. Advocacy of King's cause did not intrude upon the high-powered possibilities of the film as an early "crossover" event.

Clearly, fictional narrative film provided more opportunity for the cinematic expression of a segregated point of view, black heroes, whether pastoral or cool, and the anatomy of black society than did the documentary mode. By these standards an astonishing number of interesting black films appeared in recent years: the pastoral *The Learning Tree* and *Sounder; The Harder They Come* and *Smile Orange,* which offered Jamaican variations on American themes; *Gordon's War* and *The Spook Who Sat By the Door,* which used the anatomical mode as a means of expressing black attitudes toward urban violence; and Oscar Williams's *Five on the Black Hand Side* which attempted to depict the density of black urban life. In each case the fictional mode left the selection of incident and detail in the hands of the filmmaker rather than to the random accident of available library footage or evocative locations.

In most of these instances whatever power and conviction the movies possessed sprung from credibility built by the truths to be found in anatomical details of black life. That is, plot, incident, ambience, and character all proceeded from observation, memoir, or fictional distillations of black social life. *The Learning Tree,* for example, grew from black photographer Gordon Parks's reminiscences of rural black Kansas. Trevor Rhone's Jamaican movies rested on personal experiences and bearing witness to life in the island's recording industry and in the internecine strife among the waiters in a large hotel. Sam Greenlee's and Ivan Dixon's *The Spook Who Sat by the Door* seemed a primer for putative street fighters, an anatomy for guerrillas. *Five on the Black Hand Side* satirized anatomical details of black bourgeois life.

Each of these films borrowed from documentary style in order to fuse the reportage of visual reality with the artist's need to imitate life. Parks shot on location in Kansas. Rhone's films drew ambience from the authentic locations and awkward working conditions and facilities in Jamaica. *The Spook Who Sat by the Door* was shot on location in the streets of Gary, Indiana with the cooperation of black mayor Richard Hatcher. And *Five on the Black Hand Side* used Los

Angeles exteriors to refurbish a script intended for an East Coast ghetto. But if they exploited documentary style, they were judged as art. *The Spook Who Sat by the Door* suffered from a shrill lack of restraint that helped undermine the credibility of its gritty locations while the others wanted for better selectivity and control over detail, incident, and pacing. Nevertheless, the wider choice of imagery and materials allowed these filmmakers to create sharply etched black genre film in ways unavailable to documentary filmmakers for whom keen-edged advocacy, or propaganda, provided the main means of identity.

An exception to this apparent dichotomy which presents fictional rather than documentary film as more capable of becoming black genre might be a tiny group of musical documentaries. Because of their musical subjects, these films lent themselves to exploitation by adroit marketeers. From the earliest days of sound film, the Hollywood studios' short subjects' units had turned out two-reelers that, although they recorded actual performances of Negro orchestras, seldom reached black audiences and possessed few traits of black genre film. The style lasted until the war years when it grew into more self-consciously artful documentary trends represented by Gjon Mili's *Jammin' the Blues,* Bert Stern's *Jazz on a Summer's Day,* and others as well. Westinghouse Broadcasting and several commercial sponsors tried without success to bring the genre to television. But by the 1950s, the genre had been enervated and became dependent on one-camera setups of jazz band routines. Not until 1964, when Lee Savin and William Sargent, Jr., through an ineffective device that transferred videotape to film, brought *The TAMI (Teenage Awards Music International) Show* to the screen, did the genre revive as an exploitation of teenage markets. The formula provided the way to bring Smokey Robinson, the Supremes, and other black stars to a new audience. In 1971 D. A. Pennebaker's and Richard Leacock's *Monterey Pop* broadened singer Jimi Hendrix's market in the same way, although with greater attention to artful production values. Of the exploitation films the most patently

27. After World War II, documentaries such as Bert Stern's *Jazz on a Summer's Day* depicted more artful than political black themes. (© Bert Stern; Nederlands Stichting Filmmuseum)

black was Ed Mosk's *Soul to Soul,* an attempt to merge the markets for "soul" singles records, Ike and Tina Turner's nightclub ecstasy, and African performers, by intercutting shows performed in Africa and in the Los Angeles Coliseum.

Unfortunately for their fans, few of these musical documentaries were cinematically exciting. Mosk's *Soul to Soul,* for example, spoiled its own strategy by throwing away opportunities to cut away from performers to audiences, to cultivate the social cohesiveness expressed in the exploitation campaign.

In 1973 Mel Stuart and Columbia brought to the screen the finest attempt to make music and documentary speak to a black audience. On the surface *Wattstax* appeared to be no more than a concert on film, but actually created a genuine social ritual. The film captured a seven-hour concert in Los Angeles Coliseum that capped the annual Watts Festival. Shrewd cutting, especially to

28. Wattstax used Jesse Jackson (left) as a living symbol of its social message. (© Columbia Pictures Industries)

audience reactions, helped shape the film into more than a movie recounting a community fund raiser, but a national black ritual of unity. Less-celebrated acts intercut with a "running commentary of community people offering their views of the Black experience" were combined with footage of famous recording stars such as the Staples Singers. As a visual plea for credibility, the cutaways to the black community revealed the derelicts and defeated, as well as the celebrated and successful. The climax came through Reverend Jesse Jackson's famous black litany, "I Am Somebody," the crescendo cadence of which was paralleled by the cutting tempo. By emphasizing pride rather than aggression, *Wattstax* also invited white "crossover" audiences into the celebration. The result was the finest of a few documentary anatomies of black life in America—too few as yet to constitute a genre.

Clearly such musical and fictional anatomies of black social life have drawn larger audiences and reached higher levels of technical competence. But Carlton Moss's and Stuart Heisler's *The Negro Soldier* stands among the first films to use the documentary mode to transform anatomy into social advocacy, and deserves attention as an exemplar of the black documentary subgenre. *The Negro Soldier,* while certainly not the best black documentary, holds its place as a pioneer, not of technique like Robert Flaherty's *Nanook of the North,* but as a model of cinematic advocacy.

In retrospect the United States Army training film made in 1943 seems an unlikely wellspring of black advocacy. Indeed, because so much has happened to alter American racial arrangements since its release in 1944, the film seems dated. A few recent black audiences have received it with undisguised contempt. Nevertheless, overcoming the biases of its sponsor, the U.S. Army, at the height of World War II required such persistence and clarity of vision that the film stands as one of the finest statements of integrationist thinking ever released to a broad audience. More than any other film, *The Negro Soldier* combined black advocacy with the intelligent use of the best techniques offered by wartime Hollywood.

For many years, neither independent or government filmmakers had been attracted by Negro subjects, save for a few bits of New Deal propaganda. But with the coming of World War II, New Deal rhetoric fused with the high-flown if vague anticolonial and antiracist tone of such statements of Allied war aims as the Atlantic Charter. Even then, black critics like Claude Barnett of the Associated Negro Press found federal documentaries on racial matters "insipid."

By late 1942 the Army had determined to make film a major medium for troop training. Among its objectives was a means of dealing with deteriorating race relations in and around southern posts where whites responded to the presence of black troops with more than usual resentment and hostility. Afro-Americans had already split into factions that either refused to participate in a "white man's war" or that shared a hope for a "Double V," a simultaneous victory over foreign enemies and domestic racism. Thus the times called for a strong propaganda vehicle that spoke to black and white soldiers and civilians, giving them a reason to fight in common cause while assuaging white fears of black social gains.

Unhappy with an early script by Marc Connelly, the author of *The Green Pastures,* the Army turned to Carlton Moss, a young black worker in the Federal Theatre project. The Army initially rejected the militant ring of his first draft, *Men of Color to Arms,* eventually choosing a softer version doctored by Jo Swerling and Ben Hecht, directed by Stuart Heisler, and loosely supervised by Frank Capra, who was already caught up in the production of the famous *Why We Fight* series.

Moss knew that the segregated Army was not dedicated to leading the nation toward racial liberalism; therefore, the script necessarily prescribed a celebration of black pride of accomplishment under adversity, while deferring demands for liberal social change. Moss chose a traditional Negro church as a setting because it provided an unthreatening image for white viewers and a source of social pride and identity for blacks, and a flashback device which depicted "all the normal activities of Army life." Even then, the Army felt its "glorification" of the Negro soldier made it a "doubtful" subject for viewing by the troops. But the Army's white consultants supported Moss, even to the point of insisting on a neutral black bourgeois identity for all characters, rejecting racially identifiable dialects, dress, or manners, shouting Baptists, and "mammy" types in the flock. In the resulting debates, the even-tempered Moss seemed to Capra to be beset by "angry fervor" and wearing his "blackness like a bloody bandage." In the end Moss and the liberals won out.

The completed movie unfolded in classic studio style, set off by flawless lighting and technically perfect optical effects, and carried by a narrative in flashback. Except for its brevity and its unknown black actors, it might have been a good studio programmer that merited a week in Manhattan and a *Times* review.

A wide establishing shot puts us in a good grey gothic church. From the point of view of the congregation, we see a singing black soldier. On the last notes he is thanked by a young robed preacher played by Moss. Inspired by the song, the minister puts aside his sermon and introduces other soldiers in the pews. The example they have set calls up an allegory: in newsfilm we see black boxing champion Joe Louis regain his title from the German, Max Schmeling. The lesson is clear—in world conflict, the American way of life is at stake. A close-up of Moss reading racist cant from *Mein Kampf* is used to broaden Louis's fight into worldwide terms.

The heart of the film sketches almost two centuries of Afro-American combat drawn from historic pictures and studio reenactments: the Granary burial ground in Boston, the Boston massacre and the death of Crispus Attucks, the rebels at Concord Bridge, Bunker Hill, Trenton, and Valley Forge. The pulpit rings with the names of the black warriors. Close-ups of black and white hands building give the audience iconic reinforcement of the narrative. The march of black heroes accelerates across the years: in the Navy in 1812, at the battle of New Orleans, aboard the armored ram Monitor, in Lincoln's army, in the pioneer wagons of the westward movement, in prairie railroad gangs, on oil rigs, and in the ranks of the Buffalo soldiers during the Indian Wars.

The chronicle of American wars mounted to a well-made climax that used actual newsfilm of blacks in the Spanish-American War ("We cleaned up in Cuba," say a voiceover), of blacks digging the Panama Canal, and in a variety of roles in World War I as labor troops, *Poilus* in the French Army, the New York National Guard (which, a voiceover tells us, never lost a foot of ground nor a single soldier to enemy prisons while earning the first American *Croix de Guerre*). After the war, blacks march down Fifth Avenue where we see in close-up their two most famous heroes, Henry Johnson and

29. William Greaves's *From These Roots* revived the use of compilation footage and library stills. This photograph of a Marcus Garvey parade was taken by James VanderZee. (Courtesy William Greaves Productions)

Needham Roberts. A voiceover and a montage of monuments carries the theme into a peacetime roll call of heroes: Booker T. Washington, George Washington Carver, Matthew Henson, Jesse Owens, and the anonymous students of Howard, Hampton, Fisk, and Tuskegee.

Returning to the theme established by the Louis-Schmeling fight, the film broadens to include the Japanese, in rebuttal to the propaganda assertion that "Japan is the saviour of the colored races." One sequence centered on a black sailor at Pearl Harbor, whom black audiences would certainly take to be Dorie Miller. Miller, a steward in the segregated Navy, had leapt into a fallen deckgunner's seat and became, perhaps, the first Afro-American to fire a shot in anger in World War II.

30. *The Negro Soldier* depicted blacks in every conceivable combat role as though to symbolize a widening of opportunity that made the fight worthwhile. (War Department; Museum of Modern Art)

As though Moss's attempt to make history speak to Negroes needed an "amen," a woman rises from the flock and begins to read a letter from her son. Like other characters in the movie, she is prim and a little stiff, but projects the prescribed dignity. We cut away from her, as we did from the preacher, and follow her dutiful son through training camp, drills in the snow, and the typically segregated dance where he meets a girl. The son, like Joe Louis, personifies the black army and its new duties.

Through the soldier's letter we see improbably large numbers of Negroes in West Point, Officers Candidate School, the 99th Pursuit Squadron based at Tuskegee, black-armored cavalry outfits, and a black pilot in single combat. The son, speaking through his mother, moves the congregation to rise as one and sing a rousing "Onward Christian Soldiers" which segues into "Joshua Fi't the Battle of

31. Stuart Heisler (left) was responsible for *The Negro Soldier* from script, to screen, to previews. (War Department; Heisler Papers, Research Library, UCLA)

Jericho" and other black traditional music. The singing carries over into the upbeat ending, a split screen filled with the serried ranks of marching soldiers.

No single group of respondents unanimously admired *The Negro Soldier*. Black journalists at a preview sat in momentary silence before acknowledging its merit. While troops themselves seemed to like it, the message was so mild that only a ten percent gap separated the opinions of northern and southern white soldiers. Opinion leaders were also divided in their views: Abe Hill and Langston Hughes, two black literateurs, for example, approved, while Lawrence Reddick, curator of the Schomburg Collection, disapproved.

Even liberal white critics quarreled with the film, finding that even though it may "mean more to Negroes than most white men could imagine," its thrust was "pitifully, painfully mild." Nevertheless, despite its modulated message, the Army balked at releasing the film, thereby forcing Moss and black allies in the War Department to campaign for broad civilian distribution.

By the summer of 1944 *The Negro Soldier* had taken an early stride toward the use of documentary film as a vehicle of advocacy set in the mode of social anatomy. The movie could not be said to have radicalized America or even lectured the country on its racial duties, but it had tested an important new means of black expression. If it has endured more as a landmark event rather than a great film, it still remains an exemplar of its genre; years later its maker and the film itself provided models of racial consciousness and expression for later generations of black filmmakers and advocates. The film's vision of the anatomy of Afro-American life, its rendering of the American achievement myth as a thread of Afro-American history, and its blending of the black experience into the broader fabric of history made it a model of its genre.

7 *Nothing But a Man*

In recent years a subgenre of black film has celebrated the heroism of the picaresque outlaw who, like Sir Gawain in mortal combat with the Green Knight, Lancelot in pursuit of the Holy Grail, or Amos Tutuola's *Palm Wine Drinkard* in quest of the ultimate high, seeks himself in brave quest outside the benisons of society. The urban outlaw has especially appealed to a number of black writers. The hero of the best novel ever written by a black, Ralph Ellison's *The Invisible Man,* came from this picaresque tradition. In black genre film, this outlaw is a combative hero, who roves the city from one adventure to another, each one offering deeper rewards of both self-knowledge and gratitude from the black group in whose name he fought.

Indeed, the urban outlaw often seemed more appealing than the pastoral hero; though rural ambience provided an opportunity to sketch an anatomy of white racism, the urban scene lent itself to rich fantasies of black aggression and rebellion. John Shaft simply called forth more heartfelt response from black audiences because he scored more points against "the system" than did Br'er Rabbit.

In the midst of the recent "blaxploitation" movie cycle, filmmakers found it convenient, and even self-serving, to neglect and even demean, the less urbane pastoral hero of black folklore. For them the rural hero must have seemed too close to Uncle Tom and too much at his ease among the whites in the master class. To be on the side of the pastoral hero was somehow to acquiesce in his plight. And yet in black genre film history, a few filmmakers attempted to create a folk Negro who was his own man.

In fact, over the years the pastoral subgenre has yielded some fine movies and a few lost films with good reputations. One of the earliest black films, the Lincoln Company's *The Realization of a Negro's Ambition,* followed its prim black version of Kipps or David Copperfield from country roots to city success. While such pioneers did not start a tradition, in the 1970s when a few blacks took nominal control over a few movie projects, the genre surfaced again. Raymond St. Jacques successfully combined a fad for nostalgia and the black pastoral genre in *The Book of Numbers,* a tale which tells of small town hustlers who take on big city adversaries. Gordon Parks, Jr. reached for similar style in his near-miss biography of folksinger Huddie "Leadbelly" Ledbetter.

In the white-dominated depression years, Hollywood contributed several small black pastoral films, among them the two-reeler, *Yamacraw,* Langston Hughes's and Clarence Muse's *Way Down South,* and a string of imitators. The best Hollywood attempts—MGM's *Hallelujah!* and Fox's *Hearts of Dixie*—were among the earliest, although each was burdened by excessive sentimentality and uneven treatment of traditional black roles.

Recently the genre has enjoyed a revival through the success of four powerfully done, pictorially elegant pastoral films and an interesting liberal tract shot in the Georgia and South Carolina Sea Islands: *The Learning Tree, Sounder, The Autobiography of Miss Jane Pittman* (1974), and *Conrack* (1974). But as in earlier genres such as the hard-boiled *film noir* detective films of the 1940s, the infusion of lush financial support allowed enlargement of the sphere, variations in the form, and additions to the motifs, to such an extent that some of the films were carried outside the bounds of the genre. This is not to say the results lack former quality, but rather, former qualities.

The Learning Tree combined painterly camerawork by Gordon Parks, the natural pastoral settings of his boyhood Kansas, and a crackling narrative of a black boy initiated into the rites of passage to adulthood—all of which were the branches of Parks's "learning tree." *Sounder* similarly used pictorial beauty and rural nostalgic detail as means of nearly equalling the effect of Parks's coolly paced work. The film suffered only from its backers' too obvious wishes that it succeed financially as a "crossover" movie that would touch the sensibilities of both black and white audiences. Predictably, like a good Andy Hardy movie punched out by MGM in the 1930s, it eventually spawned a colt in the form of *Sounder II*.

The Autobiography of Miss Jane Pittman also drew its strength from pastoral roots, although its success owed less to genre formulas and more to a gimmick that allowed its story to be told through the point of view of a white reporter; the film thus qualified for viewing in the ultimate "crossover" market, the parlor audience of prime-time television. Its finest quality derived not from genre traits, but from a bravura performance by Cicely Tyson as the vigorous, open-hearted black girl, who grows to antique maturity without losing her zest for involvement in life.

Conrack was yet another colorful pastoral film. The latest of the genre was the least successful because its story rested on an ingenuous white hero imbued with a missionary spirit that many folk blacks regarded with suspicion. While Conrack is not as naively patronizing as the college student who works in a community organization only long enough to earn his three credits in "Soc. 102," he comes close. As a result, the rural black kids, their local teachers, and their gruff white supervisor are mere foils for the white carpetbagger who can risk innovation and censure because he has no permanent investment in the situation's outcome.

In the half century between *The Realization of a Negro's Ambition* and *Conrack,* the best example of black pastoral genre film was *Nothing But a Man*. A low budget, independently produced little movie shot on location in the South and New Jersey, the black-and-white, penny-pinching format did not allow deviations from generic formulas nor intrusions by well-known stars. Finite resources required that the producers rely on materials at hand, and familiar pastoral elements thus gave the film a rough-handed integrity. Straitened circumstances forced the hero to develop his character on familiar ground. Unlike the outlaw picaresque hero, the pastoral hero succeeds by keeping faith with himself, by remaining the same rather than changing, and by acquiring self-knowledge that eventually reinforces his preference for the small victory of survival with dignity. Like the hero of nineteenth-century romance, he neither kills nor is killed. In the end he may not prevail but only endure. His integrity is nonetheless preserved, because his small victories take place on a field chosen by himself—"down home" rather than in the city where, as revisionist historians are now suggesting, the integrity of the nuclear black family was destroyed by the shock of the Great Depression.

From its opening titles to its quiet ending, *Nothing But a Man* unfolds in harmony with this pastoral generic tradition. Like the myth of the eternal return, the narrative carries the hero from familiar life into inferno (the city) and then to eventual rebirth back home. The same line of incidents carries the hero's son by an earlier liaison out of the same urban blight, wrapping him too in the redemptive folds of pastoral innocence. Reinforcing this quest for the stable norms of familial heroism is the fact that the hero begins as a gandy dancer on the railroad, a monastic, nomadic life whose sterility promises none of the fulfillment possible within the family circle.

We are in a black movie, not only because the themes are black, but because our point of view is from within black circles in segregated Alabama. Whites are seen only as malevolent grotesques, omnipotent employers empowered to deny the gift of a job and wages, and polite mutes who are powerless prisoners of their racist culture. Indeed, the lines are drawn so sharply between the black and white antagonists that we need no detailed anatomy of black life to tell us who the heroes are. Nevertheless, anatomic subplots abound. During the course of the narrative, the hero is at spiritual loggerheads with his unctuous father-in-law; he wrestles between

32. In *Nothing But a Man,* the sexually segregated male world is seen as a prison from which Duff (Ivan Dixon) must escape. (Roemer-Young and DuArt; National Film Library, London)

the poles of black male freedom and domesticity; he is driven to the verge of vengeful violence, pulling back in time to keep his integrity; he descends into the wretched black city, only barely escaping its baleful forces that destroyed his own father.

Nothing But a Man opens on a black male, almost cloistered society of gandy dancers, which appears under the main titles. They work out in the flat Alabama countryside where life is hard, but as satisfying as the ring of a good hammer against steel. We are in the midst of an idyll. The camera tilts up and catches the sun; the rhythms of labor throb in time with the track workers' bending backs; their work is depicted as the central theme of their lives as the camera peers tightly down to where the hammer hits the spike.

The reality of life in a track gang, brought to us by a long fade to black and out to the interior of the bunkhouse car, is a little like a minimum security prison. There the men play fitful games of checkers with bottlecaps. One of them paces from one pal to another, picking verbal fights, hazing, and "signifying." Another worker, still in his overalls, aimlessly shaves as though to break the dullness. At last the camera tilts down on the hero, Duff Anderson —even his name has a good brown tone—paring his nails. "What are you getting pretty for?" one of the gang asks, as though to a "lifer" with nowhere to go.

At last a cut takes us outside the cloying walls, perhaps to a better place. We are on a handcar, driven along the tracks by a one-lung engine. The men are seen against the lowering sun, their heads leaning forward in anticipation against the wind. A string of truck shots catches the pineywoods, telephone poles, glinting car tops, and tidy rows of trackside shacks flickering by. Through another cut, we are in a rustic juke joint. Duff is morose. The seedy saloon is little different from the bunkcar, except for a whiney whore cadging beers. Real emotion and feeling are disguised by the poses of *aesthetique du cool*; the masks devised to conceal feelings from white men are used against black men.

Aimlessly, Duff ambles into a nighttime church service and brightens a bit at the sight, if not the message, depicted as a serial montage of warmhearted women and homey institutional ambience. The opposing life styles at last confront each other: black male celibacy versus the warm circle of black institutional family life in which respectable women have a place. After the service at a chicken supper, Duff meets Josie, the strong, cool, quietly beautiful preacher's daughter. Upstairs as the service resumes, led by a hard driving visiting preacher from Birmingham, Josie is seen as a cool quiet island amidst the cadenced black litany. A cut carries Duff outside, away from the church's light and into the dark. But we know he has been touched by the experience and that he has been drawn toward its promised affirmation.

Cutting back to the bunkhouse car or to the juke joint would have

33. Duff (Ivan Dixon) soon learns that the saloon life, populated by women for hire, offers only a cheap compromise, as visually narrow as the bunkhouse. (Roemer-Young and DuArt; National Film Library, London)

made the dichotomy into a cliché. Instead, we are made to witness a debate by being taken into the preacher's family circle where they argue about the social effect of Josie taking up with a railroad section hand. Another cut tells us she has won: a floor full of dancers seen against a backlight, and then a two-shot of Duff and Josie sipping beers. Black masculine life makes a last bid for Duff's loyalty when two of the section gang unsuccessfully intrude and try to draw him away. Duff has left celibacy for the traditional family.

Thus, in two reels Duff's place in the black world and the choices it thrusts upon him have been established. Only the introduction of his white antagonists remains. They come in the dark, hovering over Duff's parked car where he sits with Josie. His new role is thereby challenged by the whites, who press against its territorial limits and the limits of Duff's ability to protect the vulnerable blacks within his orbit. To the whites Duff is anything but a man. Indeed, they stop hazing him only when one of them identifies Josie as the preacher's daughter, and fears the wrath of some powerful white protector of the preacher. Duff is a cipher in the cracker's calculation of risk.

The incident exposes Duff's impotence against white violence and begins to threaten the pastoral family life that Josie has opened up to him. We sense it visually as they dawdle among some playground swings. Duff talks of going North. But then he says "It ain't that good up there neither." He thus rejects the city life as a solution: "Guess I belong here more than there." But ambivalence clouds his future. "They can't get you if you keep movin'," he says.

A cut takes us to Josie's house where we know her father can help only by asking Duff to become, like himself, less than a man. As though to confirm the point, there is even a white man there, the superintendent of education, who calls Duff "boy." Duff bristles, both at the white man's casual effrontery and at the preacher's safety in his protective shell within the accommodating black bourgeoisie. The power of Josie's father extends only to denying Duff access to his daughter and to offering gratuitous advice. "I think if you'd try living in a town like this instead of running free and easy you'd soon change your tune," he taunts Duff. Visually the point is made when Duff and Josie part. She stands out against the white of the verandah as Duff walks out into the rain on the way to the city and to his son. For him the price of pastoral life and its dignity is too high.

We know Josie will not give him up easily when she contrives to meet him at the bus station. But his errand is symbolically vital and he must do it alone. His son lives in a shack in Birmingham with a skinny woman who has tired of him. Duff's life becomes an episode in a long black history when the woman tells Duff of his own father's presence in the town. The quest for his son turns into a

34. Duff (Ivan Dixon) seeks out his father and finds him broken, and eventually killed, by urban life. (Roemer-Young and DuArt; National Film Library, London)

quest for his father, a drunk whose life was broken in the streets of Birmingham. Through gritty streets, up a rickety back stair, into a seedy room, Duff goes to find his father. Shabby, drunk, left arm hanging limp and useless, the man has been kept alive by a good tough woman whom he bullies and exploits. The not-yet-old man's life reaches no farther than the dirty saloon where he sometimes rests his head in the bar slop. It is clear from his example that the city promises nothing. In contrast, on the way back home, Duff is lifted by Josie's appearance, beautiful and resilient in white gloves, in the bus station.

Marriage down home, despite the opposition of Josie's father, points to a finer life than either flight to the city or escape into black male tribalism. In the long, visually powerful sequence which follows, Duff, Josie, and a linear montage of prospective white employers serve as an anatomy of black victory and defeat in the rural South. She supports him in small bits of witty badinage, intercut with scenes of painful rejection by indifferent white foremen and supers.

From marriage ceremony, to bed in a small house, to sleepy rising to face a new job, everything is closely shot with quiet intimacy, not claustrophobia. Duff's new black co-workers are less nomadic, more caught up in society, more politically aware. In his carpool they chuckle between puffs on cigars over their lame attempts to shuffle and "tom" in the proper manner. At the lumber yard the white workers serve as an anatomy of the variety of white responses to blacks. Within the limits of the movie's segregated point of view, the whites are outsiders. Nevertheless, they are seen clearly enough for Duff to distinguish between one of the them who decently surrenders the right to call Duff "boy" and another who insists on learning the details of Duff's sex life. We do not yet know how Duff will respond to his new, more stable life. We only know that he feels comfortable enough to refuse to smile to whites on demand, and to begin to think of organizing black workers into a union.

At home he finds a flurry of visual delights with intimations of black defeat off in the distance. In rapid succession there are giddy two-shots of the newlyweds exchanging gibes about sexual prowess. In their carefree sharing of taking the laundry off the line, everything is all puffs and billows of sheets and laughter, punctuated, only slightly ominously, by Josie's whimsical request for a boxing lesson for her schoolchildren. The soft scene is broken late in the day by a shrewish argument in the next cabin between a shrill wife and her husband lounging on the porch in the halflight. "You no good around the house," she snaps. Again, Duff is given a glance at cloying, psychic dangers in the black South.

Surely enough, his circle of tranquility collapses under pressures generated by his headstrong resistance to white hazing. His efforts to organize the workers are used as an excuse for a locker room confrontation in front of his more accommodating co-workers. Duff is fired and eventually blacklisted. In despair, unwilling to pick cotton, wear a bellhop's uniform, or take other "nigger work," Duff must move on.

In a montage of arch white bosses remote from the centers of black life, the film loses its black focus. Only Josie remains as a figure holding the film's center. Leave the South? "You can always do that, Duff," she says, acting as the voice which favors pastoral roots. But it is asking too much, especially when Duff must come to find her in the beauty parlor in order to borrow money to fix his car. "It's not as bad for a girl," she says. "They're not afraid of us."

The conflict between the urge for roots and desire for mobility grows. At home Josie, though pregnant and soon to lose her teaching post, volunteers to do "day work." Duff's response is to smash a chair he had been repairing in the yard. The older generation further corrupts or distorts the issue. On the one hand, Duff's father says "make them think you're going along, and get what you want." On the other, Josie's father sneers "maybe you ought to leave, . . . You'd be a lot better off in the North." Josie literally bleeds over the argument; as Duff, slumped in despair, sighs "so I've been told," she gashes her finger in the kitchen. The accident is Duff's cue to snap at her father: "You're half a man!"

Reinforcing the kinetic and verbal languages are pictures, which line the walls of their home, painted by Josie's schoolchildren. These paintings strengthen the suggestion that, despite the pounding taken by Duff, the pastoral life is verdantly fertile.

Nevertheless, Duff is broken by the pressure, at least for the moment. He shoves the pregnant Josie to the floor, and in one of the film's few fade outs, goes to Birmingham, compulsively drawn to his father's boozing half-life. Duff seems ready to surrender the last tendrils of pastoral roots for the numbing comforts of urban anomie. He ambles through the wet streets of the city, searching for his father, who first blindly rejects his son, and then dies in a drunken stupor on the way to the hospital.

Clearly, the streetscape is hell. A black funeral director blankly looks up from his desk and asks if he should "say a few words" over the dead and impersonal corpse. The dead man is the nadir of urban rootlessness: he had no age, no job, not even a birthplace. At the cemetery, a clanking backhoe, shot from a low angle, digs the nameless grave. Duff and his father's woman return from the burial through an urban wasteland like the Jersey meadows or the ashen empty landscape in Fitzgerald's *Great Gatsby*. Ancient marshes now dry, strung with utility poles and dotted with out-of-plumb tombstones are intercut with the empty faces in the car.

It is life on the bottom and Duff is touched. He decides in these depths to go back home, to "make me some trouble around town." He will even chop cotton at $2.50 per day, the job he refused when he still thought of the city as a last clear chance for salvation. His father's woman cannot believe in his rebirth. "They'll run you out," she predicts with a city dweller's skeptical shrug.

In one of the few dissolves, the filmmaker moves from urban despair toward reinvoking Duff's low key revival of faith in the pastoral scene. The dissolve is out of a one-shot of Duff turning into a rain-soaked doorway as he seeks to rescue his son from yet another generation of urban blight. He takes the boy back home in the rain, into the room where Josie's pupils' pictures line the wall, and where she receives them with wide-eyed assent. Their two-shot embraces are from a low angle, reflecting the faith in the rightness of the decision to return home. They cry as Duff reassures her: "It ain't goin' to be easy, baby. But it'll be all right."

Duff, by returning, sets himself apart from the picaresque outlaw hero who rejects his ascribed status on the bottom rung by choosing hustling opportunism rather than the integrity of home country. Duff, the pastoral hero, has learned the value of being governed by a formula that equates survival and success with sameness, roots, and permanence, rather than social mobility. Here symbol, unifying motifs, and mythic system all support the pastoral ideal of endurance. He has a vibrant country woman, who teaches the young. He

35. The scenes played between Duff (Ivan Dixon) and Josie (Abbey Lincoln) form a softly visual narrative of spiritual wholeness. (Roemer-Young and DuArt; National Film Library, London)

knows that if all else fails, he can still pick other people's cotton at least to be close to the soil. He knows he has, at the least, drawn the line by refusing to endure the extremes of humiliation at the hands of white bullies. He has even told them he will kill for the right to be "nothing but a man." To distort Faulkner, the pastoral hero does not wish to prevail, only to endure.

8 Sweet Sweetback's Baadasssss Song

Any genre should include among its subgenres some form of the heroic epic. But black film has been characterized by an absence of the hero in the tradition of El Cid, King Arthur, or even King Chaka of the Zulus. Instead, black heroic tradition, at least in the movies, has borrowed from older Afro-American traditional folk heroes, among the most influential, the trickster modelled after Br'er Rabbit or the "bad nigger" modelled after Staggerlee, the sexual outlaw of black urban folklore.

To be more precise, the urban black hero has been a "picaresque" hero in the original Spanish sense derived from the Latin; that is, a rogue or knave whose episodic fortunes are the subject of a long narrative. In still another English variant, "picaroon," the meaning is more specifically knave, brigand, and even pirate. In this sense the success of the heroic black film derives from its main character, whose outlawry and hustling a living outside the social system laid down by whites, provide a fantasy motif for naive audiences.

Of all the subgenres of black film, the picaresque, because of its facile evocation of impulsive, immediately gratifying, violent revenge fables, most lends itself to exploitation and corruption. Indeed, many of its recent exemplars have been dismissed by black and white critics alike as "blaxploitation" films, made with no more ambition than appealing to urban black youngsters by feeding their revenge fantasies. Unfortunately, like most exploitations of black taste, they concentrated on teasing their audiences rather than fulfilling their

hopes, and on exorcising the devils of the tribe rather than celebrating its beauties. Predictably, such "blaxploitation" movies soon
fell from favor and were rivaled by Oriental martial arts movies, a
new generation of science fiction monsters, and other arcana. By
1977, a major black southern university opened its spring term film
series, not with one of the ephemeral black heroes like Shaft, but
with *The Texas Chain Saw Massacre.*

After World War II few black actors combined aesthetic and box
office success with the creation of good formula movies in keeping
with the outlines of the black genre. Sidney Poitier is the best example of the distinguished, intelligent black actor whose work,
despite its quality, offered little to black fans of genre film. Indeed,
some of his movies bordered on contributing to a white generic
cinema in which the Afro-American figure was seen mainly as the
embodiment of a society where good race relations and racial integration of social life were grudgingly becoming the norm. His work
left no opportunity for other actors to develop a stark and uncompromising black picaroon; since Poitier's character had succeeded
with or without him, the picaroon's place in the postwar black film
was both needless and counterproductive.

Black intellectuals, who yearned for a blossoming black genre
film as a gimmick to stimulate mass black social and political consciousness, charged Poitier with compromising principle in exchange
for white praise. For a quarter of a century, beginning with the
United States Army training film, *From Whence Cometh My Help*
(ca. 1948), he had infused his work with a quiet, controlled in-
tensity. It was as though by an act of will, he had contained a
smouldering resentment which he had channeled into acceptable
behavior. For genre fans, that was his flaw. His heroes were ac-
ceptably cool but too reasonable and too lacking in passion for
revenge. Poitier rarely made a poor film. Indeed, his finest work,
Lilies of the Field, earned him an Oscar. But black genre fans wished
for a black hero who was more than a famous medical researcher
or diplomat, coolly superior to surrounding white society. They

wanted not merely a man apart, but a genuine black outlaw. Poitier, without success, did his best to comply in *The Lost Man* and *The Organization,* but his picaroons lacked a quick trigger finger.

On the other hand, many "blaxploitation" versions of the picaresque hero were worse than compromises. Frequently the shameless products of marketeers who teased without satisfying the deep-seated resentments of urban black audiences, the films merely choreographed violent fantasies. No one knew with certitude their impact on audiences, but black psychiatrists and social workers feared for the black children who might thoughtlessly respond to the odious stimuli in an antisocial way. The professionals, despite the occasional shrillness of their warnings, had just cause for anxiety. In almost two hundred movies, a string of witless, brutal black heroes smashed the empires and fortunes of a succession of grotesque, boorish white villains and their sexually unsatisfied white women. Unfortunately for considerations of verisimilitude, the whites bore no resemblance to the shrewd white heavies from real life. They were implausibly neurotic, sexually deviant, mindless, and insensitive. It was never clear to clever black viewers how such stupid whites had achieved so easily toppled powers.

Only occasionally "blaxploitation" movies offered good acting, tightly paced writing, and honest interracial rivalry. *Gordon's War* (1973), *Willie Dynamite* (1973), *Cool Breeze* (1972), *Melinda,* and some of Fred Williamson's movies all had their finer moments. Even then, Jim Brown's expensively mounted "crossover" movies that only superficially resembled the genre, regularly outdrew "blaxploitation" films.

By 1973 the cycle of "blaxploitation" movies was spent. In its place, Run Run Shaw and a corps of other Southeast Asian producers, who had been supplying movies to overseas Chinatowns, discovered their own formulas were those that American producers had missed or neglected.

Instead of intricate plots that ended with the shattering of Mafiosi empires, the Chinese and Singapore movies offered sure and direct revenge for personal rather than socially collective hurts. The formula rarely wavered. A good Chinese family resides in poor but happy circumstances. A Mandarin vice lord has his way with the hero's sister. She is sold into slavery. The vice lord murders the hero's parents. Up to this point, the hero has accepted his lot with diffident stoicism. But at the climax, belated according to Aristotelian formulas, he takes up his disused martial arts and slashes through a company of inept bodyguards. He fights the heavy to the death in a bloodily choreographed last reel.

No Hollywood movie depicted white heavies with such unredeeming malevolence; therefore, revenge against the white world could never be so unreservedly free of guilt. Young black audiences who watched Oriental martial arts movies could guiltlessly identify with a Chinese hero, who killed an inhumanly evil adversary, who was also Chinese. The blacks were simply once removed from the ensuing mayhem and therefore could join in the delight of rich revenge fantasies.

On the other hand, overtly universal American themes, such as the success myth of Horatio Alger, held scant appeal for young black audiences. Myths of aspiration, even during more innocent times, had lacked conviction. As early as the teens, the Lincoln Motion Picture Company had produced with marginal success *The Realization of a Negro's Ambition,* followed by Oscar Micheaux's films with their black secret agents and cops, and later in the depression, by a host of race movies featuring heroic black bourgeois success images. Best among the fables of black aspiration were *Broken Strings* (1940) with Clarence Muse's sensitive violinist, *Spirit of Youth* with Joe Louis playing himself, *Keep Punching* with Henry Armstrong's fascinating self-portrayal, Micheaux's *The Girl from Chicago* with its black federal agent, *Bronze Buckaroo* with Herb Jeffries's faithful imitation of Tom Mix, and *Gang War* with Ralph Cooper's hard-boiled Harlemite. But like the much later

Vho's Coming to Dinner, they proffered coolly successful
who overcame the barriers to upward mobility in ways that
_____available to urban blacks.

Clearly, the picaresque hero promised more direct fulfillment to
blacks on the bottom rung. Like Noble Johnson in Lincoln's half-
century-old *Trooper of Troop K,* or Ralph Cooper's slick gangsters,
the picaroon was an outlaw, both alien to the black bourgeoisie and
a victim of white cupidity, who would fight with savage directness.
And yet the formula did not allow him to vanquish every white
enemy, for his audience would surely desert him in favor of the
more stylized pleasures of the martial arts films. According to these
preconditions, Melvin Van Peebles's *Sweet Sweetback's Baadasssss
Song* exemplifies the picaresque subgenre.

Van Peebles's movie appeared on the crest of a wave of black
neo-nationalism, and therefore served, despite horrendous weak-
nesses and ambiguities, as an iconic expression of deep-seated black
resentments that flared briefly in the form of a nascent proto-national
feeling. Only months earlier, other, better-focused black movies appeared but found no black national mood with which to touch fire.
Shirley Clarke's *The Cool World* came and went, exciting only intellectuals and critics. Leroi Jones's *Dutchman* played upon black
emotions but lacked urgency or clarity. Van Peebles's own *Watermelon Man* (1970) almost spoke for a coherent mood. He had
taken a good idea by Herman Raucher—that liberalism was always
easier from a distance and involved psychic risks when practiced
in smaller circles such as neighborhood and family—and turned it
into a half-baked nationalist tract. Unfortunately garbled in transla-
tion, its resentments came from the muzzle of a blunderbuss and its
nationalism drew last reel laughter rather than black exultation or
white fear.

Van Peebles felt that *Sweetback* would be different. Out from
under major studio control, raising funds in a helter-skelter manner,
and even, so the story goes, receiving completion money from Bill
Cosby, the finished film challenged the rating system of the Motion

36. Before the relative freedom of *Sweetback,* Van Peebles learned his craft in the Hollywood studio system at Columbia Pictures. (© Columbia Pictures Industries)

Picture Association of America, insisting that the white body lacked the requisite social data to label black movies made for black audiences. It outraged blacks and whites alike, even as it exemplified the generic traits of picaresque heroism. Despite the tasteless extremes that almost guaranteed there would never be another *Sweetback,* the elements of the picaroon came through with a strength and conviction that gave shape to the black heroes of the next half-decade. It is the role of such exemplars not to be critically good so much as to point to the future.

As an exemplar of the genre, *Sweetback* exploited all the elements of the formula: a detailed and graphic social anatomy of the black underworld that established credibility; a carefully segregated point of view, which unfortunately misfired because no white character was allowed a shred of humanity; a set of symbols and gestures that bore a great freight of outlaw meaning; and a ritual of mayhem that almost orgasmically released upon the film audience the picaresque urban outlaw as a mythic black redeemer.

This is not to say the formula succeeded entirely. Van Peebles seemed to possess more conviction than experience. His anatomy of the lower depths was like that of Dostoevsky: sincere but unfounded in first-hand experience. Van Peebles was the social observer, at least as wide-eyed and astonished at what he reported as any white outsider. Moreover, Van Peebles, like John Wayne, made the title role an extension of himself, at least as modified after his flight from the world of university button-down shirts and tweeds. As Wayne's roles as the Ringo Kid in *Stagecoach* or Rooster Cogburn in *True Grit* symbolized his personal political philosophy of Jeffersonian individualism, so Van Peebles modeled his heroic role on the social rebellion expressed in his own lifestyle. But as director, Van Peebles seems only to play the role of the ghetto rebel. Like Wayne's director, John Ford, Van Peebles was the outsider, the anthropologist, who has been made an honorary member of the tribe.

From the first flicker of the opening titles, as the credits announce that the stars are "The Black Community" of Los Angeles, the viewer recognizes the anatomy of the black urban scene. As though the viewer knows that such a sentimental, overly grateful tip of the cap may seem too romantic and have a hollow ring, the main titles end with a final dedicatory line which announces that we are witnessing "a hymn from the mouth of reality." Such a deliberate confession tips us off that the movie will be set in the mode of hyperbole rather than documentary reportage. We are thus told to expect exaggeration of realistic details which invoke black group images. By magnifying observed social detail, the reportage will make anatomy serve as a sketch pad for a future black nationalist revolution, rather than an accurate view of current reality.

The opening dedication tells us that we have crossed into a revo-

lutionary combat zone: the film is for "all the black brot\
sisters who have had enough of The Man." From then\
camera carries us through a hyperbolic flight of Mau Mau rh\
laced with erotic fantasies. Indeed, according to the director,\
was the point. "The black audience finally gets a chance to see some
of their own fantasies acted out," he announced. Unfortunately, the
black audience is thus given a titillating fable of black sexuality as
a palliative for its historical political impotence. In this sense *Sweetback* was a counterrevolutionary, an enemy of the people, a mastur-
batory flight rather than a germination.

Indeed, the narrative of loosely strung episodes and alternately
flashing and shadowy images begins with sex rather than politics.
Sweetback is a black manchild-waif, taken into the social circle of
a brothel where he is nurtured, drafted into service as a sexual
instrument of the whores, and finally becomes a darkly silent sexual
performer for the titillation of the largely white patrons.

White police, in search of a patsy to spend the night in jail as a
putative suspect in a murder case, intrude and arrest Sweetback
as their suspect. Moments later, they are diverted from their mission by a radio signal to pick up a black prisoner, whom they
brutally beat under the cover of darkness. At first Sweetback watches
impassively, acting out his role as a routine arrest in the murder case.
But rage mounts within the amoral and apolitical stud, and in the
heat of the moment, he beats the cops senseless until their hand-
cuffs are dripping with blood. It is like a first step toward an eventual
conversion. The event changes Sweetback from a hustling picaroon
into a political outlaw whose consciousness intensifies with each
frame and with each picaresque episode. He had begun the film as
a political eunuch and a sexual performer. By the second reel the
roles have merged.

Sweetback's transformation experience would have been implausible but for borrowings from the genre of *film noir*. Van Peebles,
a lifelong moviegoer, saw how to use that genre's darkened streets,

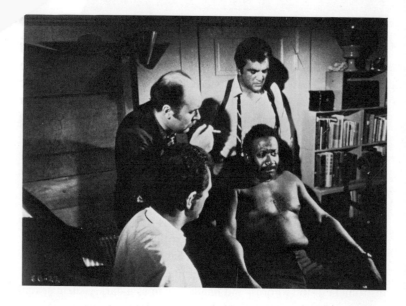

37. Sweetback's (Melvin Van Peebles) political conversion is plausible as long as cops are shown as vicious exploiters of blacks. The third-degree interrogation is the choreographed symbol of the political point. (Cinemation Industries; Museum of Modern Art)

glistening half-lights, bumbling and villainous cops. Even the raspy sound, some of it, one guesses, unintentional, contributes to the urban streetscape.

Thereafter the film is at its best when it follows Sweetback's odyssey from picaresque whimsies to political awareness, and at its worst when hyperbolic sex-linked violence triumphs over the political thread. We see, for example, his growing sense of outlawry through the eyes of his own people, those who must take the risks if urban guerrillas can expect to win. At an early high point they ostracize him as a "dead man" and send him off with a parable-toned last supper of the condemned.

Nevertheless, such hyperbole and exaggeration become no more than clever throwaway lines unless they emerge from a plausible set-

38. Sweetback's (Melvin Van Peebles) relationships with blacks, including the prostitutes he is used by, are almost vulnerable and human.
(Cinemation Industries; Museum of Modern Art)

ting of anatomical social reality. It was the reason for the popular
success of George Orwell's *1984* and for the failure of the movie
version of it. Van Peebles knew something of this and created a tour
de force of visual signals, of grainy tableaux of vacant lots, trashy
street scenes, parti-colored by paint-peeling graphics hanging from
disused storefronts. In the backrooms, storefront churches, and on
street-corners, we see the defeated and passive blacks, who hustle
each other as though a reminder of the beginnings of Sweetback's
journey.

It becomes more clear that Sweetback is maturing from picaroon
hero into the classic mode of the sojourner on a holy quest. We
might even anticipate that he will go forth into the wilderness (although to expect him to build a votary chapel would be stretching

the point). The movie makes good use of a fragile lacework of images that could easily crumble, as long as Sweetback survives in the city within black circles. The film stumbles only when, like St. Augustine, he goes into the desert in flight from society, there to be purified by the experience. It is here that the movie loses its point deep in the southwestern desert, remote from the community whose plight presumably concerns us.

Out in the yellow broken hills, the premise goes astray and Sweetback's simple nationalist politics bloat into a self-indulgent fantasy. Like Marlon Brando, John Barrymore, or Lon Chaney indulging themselves by playing twisted, ugly roles Van Peebles/Sweetback has become a Simon of the Desert, loping down the dry concrete bed of the Los Angeles River and into the crags where he feeds off the live raw denizens of the rimland. Politics give way to narcissism. Symbolically, the movie has ended. The black community has been deserted. Sweetback jogs from one disconnected escapade to another, brushing against groups of migrant Mexican pickers, riding atop rickety busses, pausing only for a heroic display of sexual prowess that brings a pagan motorcycle-gang mamma to screaming orgasm.

Away from the city even the pungent white heavies suffer for want of persistence and constancy of image. Not only has the black urban *lumpenproletariat* been abandoned; the white heavies and degraded troglodytes, who had fed off the sexual aberrations in the whorehouse, the brutalities casually inflicted by the police, and the delectable humiliations thrust upon weak and helpless Afro-Americans, have also disappeared.

Both black and white images were central to the film's political point. Absent and half-remembered, they render the movie pointless. We recall, not a white racist social system, but rather vague, one-dimensional, wet-lipped decadents leering in brothels, and sadistic cops, who rightfully die in their flaming squad cars—all of them perfect *Horror Comix* cartoons that teach us nothing. The blacks, more naturalistic and less exaggerated, are less interesting, and Van Peebles easily sheds them for the fantasies of the desert. He becomes Pasolini shooting *The Gospel According to St. Matthew* (1964), taking the movie into the desert where he elects himself Christ, dedicates the future of blacks to his second coming, and thereby inadvertently castrates the present-day black masses for whom he has claimed so much anarchic social strength. Like Elia Kazan's *Viva Zapata* (1952), the Hollywood biography of Mexican revolutionary, Emiliano Zapata, *Sweetback* has given blacks only a wraith to pray for and denied them all hope except that which resides in himself, and his promised but improbable return. Protesting too much his vengeful return to the black community, and as though the rhetoric of the cinema fails to convey such highflown messages, Sweetback's last baleful message promising his return is superimposed over the frame like a thirty-second television spot made for a used-car dealer.

This is not to say *Sweetback* plays its audience entirely false. Almost subliminal images which jog against the message of the movie suggest that Van Peebles, despite frequent cocky disclaimers, was sincere, if not in command, of the medium of cinema. One example illuminates this point. A cadenced black preacher's sermon becomes the occasion for first hinting at *Sweetback's* messianic demiurge; it is all plausible because at the time *Sweetback* is, like an urban guerrilla, still concealed from view deep within black haunts. But it is as though Van Peebles is unsure he can maintain the power of such images using only the mode of social realism.

Later when he has an opportunity to restate the message in allegorical terms (acceptable to black mass audiences because it conformed to legends of black sexual prowess), he throws aside the chance. The incident begins during his sexual adventure among a gang of white motorbikers, which was intended to cast Sweetback into an aggressive symbol of black sexuality. Instead, Sweetback mounts the skinny white woman, servicing her in plodding, conventional missionary style. The prosaic wide-shot can arouse nothing in the woman or the audience. Van Peebles then abandons the mode al reality that has characterized the early reels, substituting __.ed, jangling, negative prints over which we hear her too shrill orgasmic scream. Sweetback, it becomes clear, is not a sexual messiah at all, but merely an adolescent streetcorner braggart.

Nevertheless, *Sweetback* remains an extremely useful black genre film, not only because of its consistent use of the cool-handed black outlaw and other genre traits, but also because so many genre variants were stimulated by the film's splashy financial success. Thus the point is not whether it entirely succeeds in being faithful to its own romantic political convictions. True, the lone ending in the desert, when it seems to promise an eternal return, rings false. But the movie, like Vidor's *Hallelujah!,* remained on target as long as Van Peebles fixed on the setting that formed the premise of the movie. Vidor's pastoral sequences and Van Peebles's ghetto footage both ring true. Yet, when each shifted focus to another locale, their films misfired.

Nonetheless, in the early going, *Sweetback* maintains a pointedly segregated focus through which racial politics may be seen with particular vividness. The film's symbols of white oppression and black defeat, by virtue of their heavy-handed caricature quality, depersonalize revenge motives in a manner similar to a martial arts movie. Of all the "blaxploitation" movies, *Sweetback* was most able to convey a dirt poor ghetto ambience with startling conviction. Thus, as a social anatomy of the poor black lower depths, it is without peer, at least in its early reels. Therefore, as long as Sweetback remains in the city, he stands tall as an outrageous symbol of the loser who impulsively strikes back. And as long as he is in control of the situation in his small circle, he speaks to his audience through the fluid, easy-riding mode of the *aesthetique du cool* style adapted by urban youth. Following its release that this generation of black audiences spent millions seeking its sequel in two hundred cheap imitators is testament to the film's power, despite its empty promises of redemption by a tin black Christ.

Criticism and Scholarship

Black film has not been blessed with a critical tradition, merely celebrants or traducers, worshippers or infidels. For reliable knowledge, systematic standards of appreciation, and methodical criticism, only a few recent historical essays will serve the interested observer. At that, much of the literature still is tinged with plagiarism, preciousness, and cheerleading. Present-day students of film are necessarily the leading edge of an eventually more sophisticated criticism.

During the heyday of independent black filmmaking only a few theatrical critics in the northeastern metropolitan Negro press took an interest in race movies. The NAACP and other organizations with middle-class constituencies stood apart, neither endorsing black films, nor using them as the occasions for fund-raising benefits. Many professional black actors found the films regressive and ineptly done, and therefore turned to Hollywood films as a standard of professional success. Thus, in the formative years after 1916, this lack of middle-class and professional attention to race movies discouraged the growth of a written critical tradition. The few Afro-American newspapers that broke the silence usually had a vested interest in the films, either because their film and theater critics also served as theatrical bookers, their papers sought advertising revenue from theater owners, they built greater newsstand sales that accrued from covering premieres, or, as in the case of the *Pittsburgh Courier,* a marriage of convenience with a film company.

Not only did film criticism begin late, but most of it consisted of editorials directed against white movies about Negroes. The first black film criticism appeared in the August, 1929, issue of *Close Up,* a little magazine founded in Switzerland by Kenneth MacPherson, Winifred Bryher, and other American expatriates, whose aesthetic interests included the future of Negroes in films. Their authors included Afro-Americans, Marxist critics such as Harry Allan Potamkin, and the aesthetes themselves, who put together a little film called *Borderline* (1930), starring Paul and Eslanda Goode Robeson. An atmospheric fable about the impact of racism on two Ne-groes in a Swiss village, it was designed to illustrate their belief in the need for a black cinema. The issue, coming as it did on the eve of Hollywood's release of *Hearts in Dixie* and *Hallelujah!*, signaled a rush of comment on motion pictures in such serials as the Urban League's *Opportunity,* the NAACP's *Crisis,* the fan magazine *Photo-play,* the radical *Liberator,* and the *New York Times.* This outpour-ing not only marked the beginning of criticism of black film, but in its merging of aesthetics and social import, outstripped most of the criticism of the succeeding decade.

A mid-Depression revival of black imagery on the Hollywood screen inspired not only a rejuvenation of race movies but a re-sumption of criticism; unfortunately for black independents, how-ever, the approach was heavily paved with liberal progressivism. Only William Harrison's "The Negro and the Cinema," in the dis-tinguished British journal *Sight and Sound* (1939) and James Asendio's brief piece in *International Photographer* (1940), held out hope for a unique black film tradition.

The 1940s' critics, caught up as they were in the spirit of Allied war aims with their veiled promise of an end to colonialism and racism, turned away from black films to Hollywood movies full of tales of racial integration and good race relations. The best of them followed the line of Alain Locke's and Sterling Brown's appreciative essay on Hollywood's use of black folklore in *Hallelujah!* and *Hearts in Dixie*: they searched each new movie for fresh signs of progress. Locke and Brown, along with other black intellectuals and Oscar DePriest, the black Chicago congressman, had regarded these two Hollywood musicals as landmarks of a sort, clearly breaking fresh ground, but also to be regarded warily for fear of their eventually pointing backward to the ruts of the Southern past.

The critics of the 1940s carried the two black scholars a step further by calling for a Hollywood cinema that would change Ameri-can attitudes by destroying the race-linking of Negroes to a few narrowly conceived vices, and by opening up the screen to treatment of Negroes "like everybody else." The result, in the view of Lawrence Reddick, the best spokesman of this libertarian point of view, would be a decent and civil cinema that would improve race relations and pave the way for an egalitarian future free of the constraints of traditional racism.

Reddick, the curator of the A. A. Schomburg Collection of Afro-Americana in the 135th Street Branch of the New York Public Library, must be counted as the first black critic who applied scholarly standards to his work. Largely because of the Schomburg's judicious collecting of clippings on Negro show business, Reddick was able to survey almost on a daily basis the black contribution to American popular art. His essay in a 1944 issue of the *Journal of Negro Education* appeared in the heat of the mid-war riots in Harlem, just after the wartime bargaining between NAACP leaders and the Hollywood studio chiefs. These meetings led him to hope for an integrated future, so imminent that it could be plotted in seven neat steps. For him, therefore, "the strategy of working for better treatment of the Negro, accordingly, must be worked out in terms of the profit motive of the industry and not through Jim Crow black movies." Thus, in the end, Reddick and his generation left little room for the growth of an independent black film industry. Nevertheless, their work was instrumental in defining standards of excellence, even if tainted with too much insistence on "positive images."

In the next few years, a number of young critics emerged to refine Reddick's sociology of film art. More than any other generation of writers on black themes, they hammered the point that segregation on racial lines created barriers of ignorance that perpetuated the creation of racial stereotypes, each to serve as a deeper wedge between two races, whom history had separated, but whom liberalism could bring together. They regularly appeared in the black press, the *New York Times,* and the Marxist press, and by the end of the wartime decade and the decade of integration that they had helped bring about, they began to appear in books and in scholarly quarterlies. If they did little to serve black film, they at least effectively called for a restructuring of Hollywood priorities.

Curiously, the critic who came to be accepted as the *beau idéal* of the period was Peter Noble, a young Englishman. Noble's *The Negro in Films* (1948) provided footnotes for a later generation of self-conscious black critics, whose potted surveys accepted as gospel his often impressionistic data and naive generalizations. Nevertheless, he gave some attention to black filmmakers, at least in his filmography, which was larger than any published before 1948.

Even less founded on empirical data, and marred by an unquestioning faith in Marxist dialectics was V. J. Jerome's *The Negro in Hollywood Films* (1950). Nevertheless, Jerome, too, kept alive the concept of a black cinema by using the inadequacies of Hollywood's postwar crop of racial themes, presented as social problems, as occasion to call for a doctrinaire Marxist black nationalist solution to "the Negro question." His indictment of soft liberalism for its inability to move to the conclusions necessitated by the exposure of racism called attention to the continuing need for a black independent cinema. Jerome's close analysis of Hollywood's message movies still merits attention for its finely focused eye for social detail. In contrast to Jose Yglesias, his able contemporary on the *Daily Worker,* Jerome could convey argument without precasting it in rigid Marxist terms.

In the 1950s, such diverse critics as Ralph Ellison, Gerald Weales, James Baldwin, and the shamefully neglected Albert Johnson, wrote pointedly, and often without apparent immediate impact, on the need for a black cinema in the face of Hollywood's failure to move beyond the Negro as an isolated figure in a white landscape) If the integrationist era did not seem ripe for a careful definition of black cinema, at least the inadequacies of integrationist cinema did not go unnoticed. Moreover, unlike some generalists of the war years, these critics focused their attention on specific, and often highly praised, liberal films such as *Intruder in the Dust, Carmen Jones,* and *Island in the Sun.* More than at any time since *Close Up,* black critics intruded on a white critical preserve, this time in magazines of larger, more sophisticated readership such as *Commentary* and *Film Quarterly*. Baldwin and Ellison brought their intelligence to the problems of evaluating individual films—though with unfortunate infrequency—while Johnson, especially in his durable "Beige, Brown or Black" in *Film Quarterly* (1959), and Martin Dworkin in his two long essays in the *Progressive* (1959–1960), surveyed the shifting styles of the entire period.

But by the early 1960s, with Hollywood in a state of flux, independent production migrating abroad, and black filmmaking stifled by Hollywood's misreading of Sidney Poitier's successful career, no systematic school of historical or critical principles emerged. Careful chronicling of the narrative history of black filmmaking devoid of analysis or theory, agreement on a few broad liberal principles of social change and their reflection on the screen, and a faith in the eventual racial integration of American life seemed enough. Critics seemed content to reach a liberal consensus made possible by avoiding probing controversies beneath the surface of progress.

Then in February 1969, Hoyt Fuller published in his annual black history issue of *Negro Digest* an essay meant to urge critics to examine this neglected Afro-American film history. Unfortunately, the primitive essay on "movies in the ghetto" was taken by many to be an "amen," rather than a timid beginning. Mention was made, for example, of Emmett J. Scott, Booker T. Washington's secretary, and his desire to make black films; yet Scott's papers remain unsifted fifty years later. Only a few articles published since 1969 have examined any of the companies cited in the piece. Instead of its intended modest purpose, it became merely a strip mine from which to cull program notes, footnotes, and in some cases, whole passages.

For three years, the only exception to this rule was Stephen F. Zito's "The Black Film Experience" in Tom Shales's impressionistic book, *The American Film Heritage,* designed as a showcase of American Film Institute acquisitions. Zito's essay, though sketchy in keeping with the tone of the book, attempted to indicate the close and necessary connection between social intentions and the success of black movies, as opposed to the fruitlessness of seeking some purely artistic ground for analysis. According to Zito, an unlikely combination of a Viennese director "at liberty," a German immigrant searching for something to do between hack works at Columbia Pictures, a black performer working nights on Broadway in *Lost in the Stars* while earning a few daylight dollars in *Miracle in Harlem,* were the prime movers and shapers of black genre movies, at least in the 1940s. Their films were frequently uneven victims of caprice, circumstance, and accident, rather than conscious works of art.

Still, no great wave of black film analysis followed Zito's line of attack. Edward Mapp's book of the same era, *Blacks in American Films,* lacking a critical point of view, makes no mention of Micheaux or his rivals and introduces Leroi Jones's *Dutchman* as merely "another 1967 film to have a subway car as its setting." Shirley Clarke's films on blacks and Van Peebles's *Sweetback* all are presented with studied neutrality that skirts the issue of genre.

By 1973 critical and historical writing still held more promise than attainment. Only one major performing figure, Paul Robeson, had been treated in a scholarly article. Only two black companies, the *Birth of a Race* Company and the Lincoln Company, had been examined across the years of their productive lives. Only a handful of black genre motion pictures had ever been analyzed in full articles —*Native Son, Scar of Shame, Sweetback, Up Tight* (1968), *Nothing But a Man, Book of Numbers.* Only a handful of directors have been interviewed in circumstances free of constraints imposed by calls for timeliness or "relevance"—Ossie Davis, Van Peebles, Michael Roemer, St. Clair Bourne, Madeleine Anderson. Only one essay of stature, Pauline Kael's long *New Yorker* piece, has examined with insight a subgenre, "blaxploitation" pictures.

In Europe a similar myopia prevailed. *Blacks in the Cinema*: *The Changing Image,* a British Film Institute pamphlet by Jim Pines that grew into a book, barely mentioned race movies in its filmography, mislabeling at least one of them as a "Hollywood" film, while granting that liberal movies failed because they "couldn't develop beyond the notion of 'equality.' " In French criticism, reviewers have focused mainly on jazz on film.

Then a retrospective of black movies by the Jewish Museum in New York resulted in university campus echoes of interest, culminating in a traveling series produced by Oliver Franklin of the University of Pennsylvania's Annenberg Center for Communication Arts and Sciences. Popular pictorial histories began to find room for black films. Eileen Landay's *Black Film Stars* (1973), although spoiled by its narrow focus on glamorous types, gave a few pages to Micheaux and his contemporaries. Middleton Harris's *The Black Book* (1974) enhanced its rough scrapbook quality with photographs of race movie posters.

Serious writers began to mature in their analysis of the relationship between white society and emerging black film. Charles D. Peavy's important piece buried in the back of Ray Browne's *Popular Culture and the Expanding Consciousness* (1973) did more than any other essay to point out the curious relationship between rising black cinema awareness and its white foundations. Thomas Cripps attempted a similar correlation between white television stations and black audiences in the *Journal of Popular Culture.* James P. Murray, film critic for the *Amsterdam News* and an editor of *Black Creation,* sponsored by the New York University Institute of Afro-American Affairs, assembled his thoughts on black cinema consciousness into an awkward but enthusiastic appeal for a search "To Find An Image." The goals of new black cinema, he argued, were to correct white distortions, to reflect black reality, and to create a "positive image." Gordon Parks, Melvin Van Peebles, Ossie Davis, William Greaves, and St. Clair Bourne were those who promised a black future for filmmakers.

Among recent critics, two anthologists, Richard A. Maynard and Lindsay Patterson, brought together fugitive essays from the past (though never from far enough back to rescue pioneering black newspaper critics, such as Lester Walton, Romeo Daugherty, D. Ireland Thomas, and Floyd Snelson from oblivion). Maynard's *The Black Man on Film* (1974), a sampling of works on the general topic of racial stereotyping, managed to include in the selection process trenchant pieces such as Ossie Davis's essay on the making of *Purlie Victorious*; Reddick's anatomy of good cinema race relations; essays on *The Birth of a Nation*; popular estimates of new black movies; and a rescuing of Baldwin's and Ellison's film essays from undeserved elusiveness.

Patterson's collection was more self-conscious in its search of a "great tradition," and like Murray's book, more directly concerned with advocacy of a new black cinema. His older authors included Locke and Brown, Reddick, a bit from the black issue of *Close Up,* Harrison's *Sight and Sound* piece, Albert Johnson, and Asendio, among others. In each case he juxtaposed them opposite recent critics who insisted on a new black cinema, sometimes with weighty argument, sometimes with nothing more than shrill enthusiasm. In an introduction in the form of a note to his son, he openly demonstrated his advocacy by describing his book as "a superb account of the road we've already traveled and are yet to travel, cinematically."

Intended almost as a kind of summary of and a call for a larger corpus of new black film criticism, *Black Creation* devoted its 1973 winter issue to new black film. Here, too, the ambition was to connect present self-consciousness with past pioneering, through essays which emphasized the need for fresh sources of capital, black film as "a tool for liberation," and by Murray's "futuristic fable" about the heady times that might bring about a new black film industry. The issue began with Pearl Bowser's sketch of the half-hidden past of Noble Johnson, Oscar Micheaux, and Paul Robeson—the elusive great tradition—a wide-eyed, head up "History Lesson: The Boom is Really an Echo."

But great traditions demand great syntheses, which rest on a body of systematic criticism. That task, among critics of black cinema, still remains. Two book-length studies appeared: the former,

Toms, Coons, Mulattoes, Mammies, & Bucks: An Interpretive History of Blacks in American Films by Donald Bogle, at the crest of the new wave of black interest in the screen; the latter, *From Sambo to Superspade: The Black Experience in Motion Pictures* by Daniel J. Leab, surfaced at a point of possible summation of the movement toward a black cinema. Nevertheless, each left open the final question of how to deal with a film genre that is proudly more social than artistic, more political than subtle, more given to advocacy than to nuance.

Of the two books, Bogle's came closest to offering a systematic method of criticizing black film while avoiding the intellectual trap of too fine an aestheticism. But, unfortunately for serious students, he turned his eye for pregnant detail on the tricks and quirks that black performers used to enhance, humanize, and enlarge the stereotyped roles given them by Hollywood writers imprisoned by racist history and culture, to the exclusion of a careful, methodic anatomy of the movies.

While it is true for the first time Micheaux's work received a chapter, it was titled merely "The Interlude." Bogle was clearly happiest at the enjoyable task of puncturing the pink bubbles sent aloft by Hollywood studios. There seemed to be no room for a methodic analysis of aberrant film, such as Vidor's, Dudley Murphy's, or Shirley Clarke's, or for the outlaw tradition of race movies.

The black gems which existed amidst the dross of the "blaxploitation" era were seen as qualified successes, or at their worst, as rehashes of old stereotypes. In the case of Van Peebles's *Sweetback,* Bogle preferred to carefully report the sociology of movie attendance, reviewing, and attitudes, resulting in a safe evaluation of the film as "a striking social document on the nature and attitudes of the new era." Similar films such as Sig Shore's *Superfly* (1972) were also given judgements that were more moral than methodic. *Superfly* seemed merely "corruptive." This is not to say that Bogle's useful insights were totally lacking. Fragile and interesting ideas, such as a parallel between *Sounder* and *Hallelujah!*, unfold. As a result, *Toms, Coons, Mulattoes, Mammies & Bucks* remains the first serious effort to update and Afro-Americanize Noble's 1948 work, *The Negro in Films*.

Daniel J. Leab's *From Sambo to Superspade* followed Bogle's book and brought to black film criticism the craft of the historian. But Leab, too, skirted the question of method in studying black film, first by finding nearly every black appearance in white film to be no more than puppeteering, and second, even though granting the constraints imposed by cheap budgets, by emphasizing standards of quality rather than meaning when appraising race movies.

Nevertheless, *From Sambo to Superspade* reached behind the screen to the social and economic forces that shaped the image presented to audiences. Unfortunately, the preoccupation with "image"—the caste mark of many authors who urge a progress toward the "positive"—diverts attention away from methodic standards of judgment and evaluation of black films. But the serious student should not ignore either Bogle's personal vision of black film history or Leab's historical approach.

It would be useless to find the literature wanting, unless an alternative is offered. Among the possibilities is Andrew Tudor's synthesis of the sociology of cinema in *Image and Influence*. If most forms of culture are sources of identity, aspiration, technique, and escape, he says, then the close observer should be able to understand film as an expression of these urges. Thus the study of the black film genre furthers the degree to which the student follows Herbert Gans's notion that the audience interacts with, and affects, the filmmaker. Therefore a mechanism exists through which either a black or white filmmaker may make a black film based upon his ability to perceive and respond to artistic and mythic needs of an audience.

Unfortunately, perhaps because of the implied manipulation of attitudes, serious students of film have frequently felt uncomfortable applying the technique to other than authoritarian societies, as though it was acceptable for Siegfried Kracauer, David Stewart Hull, and Lotte Eisner, to make this discovery about Nazi German film-makers but not about American filmmakers. Despite this scholarly holding at arms' length, Tudor's macro-sociology (as he would call it) of film allows the critic to perceive culture patterns in films, and thereby to appreciate both the genre and the society that produced it. As Tudor says of Kracauer, "his real aim is to see the early years of the German cinema as a *monologue interieur* giving access to '. . . almost inaccessible layers of the German mind.' " While Tudor's is a true statement of our goals, we want a keener understanding of the films, rather than the mind.

The matter of style serves as an example. It is common knowledge that German expressionism, with its twilight of lights and darks, expressed moody alienation from the outer civilization that had rejected the German nation as well as National Socialism's inexorable embrace of comforting authoritarianism. What of black film style? A look at any early black film reveals a self-evident segregation from white life. A closer look reveals, whether in a roughly shot Micheaux film or the polished *The Scar of Shame,* flat and grey interiors lacking visual reference to a world outside the tiny sets, internalized, looking at themselves, without need of a peephole into the white world. Too much may be claimed for stylistic devices that serve as the signature of auteurs. Lewis Milestone's famous truck shots of troops mowed down by machine gunners was no more than a cost-cutting gimmick. In like manner, in race movies the blacks knew they were segregated and so did their occasional white directors, who had a distinct feeling of straying into another world. Thus, cliched one- and two-shots against a gray wall, or parallel cutting to a jivey dance routine in some seedy Negro saloon, were signals of black society in a motion picture frame. To blacks they meant "this movie is about 'us' " and was shot in private. *Wattstax,* through the use of the Los Angeles Coliseum, and *The Spook Who Sat By the Door,* with its introductory anatomy of black bourgeois cultural experiences, evoke the same image.

In the same way, certain thematic obsessions reflect the concerns of Afro-American society. "Making it," getting on in society, is a never ending theme, whether via the great leaping, click of the heels as Thalmus Rasulala in *Cool Breeze* knows he has accomplished what Emmerich and Riemenschneider failed to do in *The Asphalt Jungle* (1950) version; or in Micheaux's light-skinned women, who will accept a beating from a man who seems a winner, but would die before giving money to a loser.

Put together over a number of years, the combination of cool ambience, isolation, aspiration, faith in rackety jazz routines to perk up flagging audiences and to stretch out the length of films to marketable running times, and even the mandatory depiction of a bitter suspicion of out-group antisocial forces (gangs, racketeers, scam-artists who populate Ralph Cooper's Manhattan movies as surely as they later would Richard Roundtree's) add up to a relatively fixed pattern of symbols than can, and should, be studied as a genre. As Tudor holds: genres represent a kind of evolution—a " 'survival of the popular.' Bit by bit communicators produce new variations, audiences accept or reject them, they are continued or discarded, and so the genre slowly evolves." In this sense neither MGM nor Gordon Parks made *Shaft*; he emerged from a subculture whose parents had seen or heard of Ralph Cooper in *Dark Manhattan*.

But genre must be distinguished from mere exploitation movie. A genre emerges from many films, gradually refined to appeal to a persistent collective taste. Some are good while others are bad, according to standards of aesthetics as well as by the formal, though unarticulated, standards of the genre. John Huston's *The Maltese Falcon* (1941), for example, may be judged as the finest film ever made of its genre, while failing to measure up to the prevailing standards of dramatic film criticism. The genre demands of its creators a faithfulness to the collective spirit and psychic needs of the audience. On the other hand, the exploitation film derives its identity more from the tastes of a narrow, arcane audience who are appreciative of forbidden pleasures or eccentricities. Such an audience is drawn to, say, "skin flicks" or Yiddish films, each for different reasons, but for common types of pleasure. In this sense, genres are like tribal rituals invoking familiar beauties; exploitations are like satanic rites glimpsing devils. Of course, these broad generalizations can sometimes go too far. Carlos Clarens, for example, argues from assertion rather than persuasive data, that horror films are really expressions of deep-seated "Jungian" collective obsessions.

Thus the argument for the existence of genres speaks to the issues of tone, scene, texture, theme, and message rather than technique. In the black genre, for instance, a segregated point of view, familiar symbols, close anatomical details, and myth offered in cool style provide signs of identity. Filmic devices matter, but are not unique, to the genre. A wide pan shot appears in many movies. In *War and Peace* (1956), it takes in a ballroom and its doomed dancers; in *South Pacific* (1958), a blue horizon; in *She Wore a Yellow Ribbon,* a ridge over which a Cheyenne war party will ride. The kind of shot and its length are merely tools; it is the content that is generic. Of course, some shots lend themselves to certain genres. Why move the company to Monument Valley, only to overuse tight closeups that minimize the sweep of the terrain?

The western genre is about the tensions between society and individual, West and East, wilderness and civilization. Thus the lone gunman, who lives by the Western variant of the antebellum Southern *code duello,* is important to the genre and so invites the artistic conclusion that he must be shot, reed-slim, and stark against the low hills at the end of the dusty Western street. One step further on, the fact that the genre requires him to shoot it out with his grizzled enemy over a minor point of honor, is more important to the genre than how the scene will be shot, though again, certain shots and rhythms will suggest themselves to a sensitive director. Indeed, the western or any other genre almost forces the use of certain stylized shots, cuts, and rhythms, the line between genre film and cliché being necessarily thin. In the same way, the gangster film's ambience of wet, dark streets and the themes of grasping individualism outside the laws of indifferent "straight" society symbolize a fatalistic adherence to private codes of morals and anomic urban aloneness. Here, too, the film's devices merely service the content.

Finally, that is where the critical literature of the black film genre must go: toward a synthesis of ritual, myth, social meaning, toward those preaesthetic judgments that measure the ability of film genres in Tudor's words, to "dramatize, repeat, and underline an interpretive account of acceptable social order." Furthermore, we must seek black film as a special case of genre film. We are told that genre film has been conservative in its ideology, although black film demands change. But because black filmmakers insist that black heroes win against the system, it can be argued that the black hero symbolizes a wish for things as they are—a permissive society whose libertarian political values allow him a temporary defeat of its elitist racist social system.

Thus, rather than the norms of life, the black genre should be expected to depict deep within its syntagmas, its value-laden images, its allegories, its icons, the outlaw, the obsessed, the deviant, the heroically fantastic. Such a critical future might logically make use of several cultural approaches: the holistic grasp of the central mythic continuities of a culture; the structural-linguistic quest for anthropological meanings of Claude Lévi-Strauss and Christian Metz; or the approach from popular culture with its emphasis on mass audience responses and value-laden formulas.

Bibliography

ALEXANDER, FRANCIS W. "Stereotyping as a Method of Exploitation in Films." *Black Scholar* VII (May 1976): 26–29. An example of black interest in film criticism.

ARMAS, JOSE. "Antonio and the Mayor: A Cultural Review of the Film." *Journal of Ethnic Studies* III (Fall 1975): 98–101. One of the many essays on other ethnic groups' dissatisfaction with depictions in popular film.

ASENDIO, JAMES. "History of Negro Motion Pictures." *International Photographer* II (January 1940): 16–17.

BENNETT, LERONE, JR. "The Emancipation Orgasm: Sweetback in Wonderland." *Ebony* XXXVI (September 1971): 106–08. An example of the controversy stirred by the new black movies.

BOGLE, DONALD. *Toms, Coons, Mulattoes, Mammies, & Bucks: An Interpretive History of Blacks in American Films.* New York: Viking Press, 1973.

BOWSER, PEARL. "The Boom is Really an Echo." *Black Creation* IV (Winter 1973): 32–35. Brief, derivative, interesting history of race movies between the World Wars.

BROWN, ROSCOE C. "Film as a Tool for Liberation?" *Black Creation* IV (Winter 1973): 36–37. A special pleading for a broader participation by blacks in filmmaking.

CAWELTI, JOHN G. "Notes Toward an Aesthetic of Popular Culture." In *Popular Culture and the Expanding Consciousness,* edited by Ray B. Browne. New York: John Wiley, 1973. A tentative suggestion that the auteur theory of film criticism may enrich the evaluative tools of popular culture critics.

———. *The Six-Gun Mystique.* Bowling Green, Ohio: Bowling Green

University Popular Press, 1971. A traditional study of the western, combining literary and sociological techniques.

COLEMAN, HORACE W. "Melvin Van Peebles." *Journal of Popular Culture* V (Fall 1971): 368–84.

CRIPPS, THOMAS. *Black Shadows on the Silver Screen. Post-Newsweek* Television, Ray Hubbard, Executive Producer, 1975. A one-hour television compilation-film that surveys the history of race movies.

———. "The Birth of a Race Company." *Journal of Negro History* LIX (January 1974): 28–37.

———. "The Death of Rastus: The Negro in American Films Since 1945." *Phylon* XXVIII (Fall 1967): 267–75.

———. "The Lincoln Motion Picture Company and the *Birth of a Race* Company: Two Early Strides Toward a Black Aesthetic." In "Film and Africana Politics" (mimeo), edited by Harold Weaver, Jr. New Brunswick, N.J.: Department of Africana Studies, Rutgers College, Rutgers University, 1973, pp. 1–26.

———. "The Movie Jew as an Image of Assimilationism, 1903–1927." *Journal of Popular Film* IV (3): 190–207.

———. "Movies in the Ghetto Before Poitier." *Negro Digest* XVIII (February 1969): 21–27; 45–48.

———. "Native Son in the Movies." *New Letters* XXXVIII (Winter 1972): 49–63. One of a very few analyses of an individual black movie and its maker.

———. "The Noble Black Savage: A Problem in the Politics of Television Art." *Journal of Popular Culture* VIII (Spring 1975): 687–95. An attempt to show that a countervailing and decisive black influence upon a popular medium raises as many new problems as it solves old ones.

———. "Paul Robeson and Black Identity in American Movies." *Massachusetts Review* XI (Summer 1970): 468–85.

———. *Slow Fade to Black: The Negro in American Films, 1900–1942.* New York: Oxford University Press, 1977.

DWORKIN, MARTIN. "The New Negro on the Screen." *Progressive* XXIV (October-December 1960): 39–41. A useful survey of postwar black roles in Hollywood films.

FRANKLIN, OLIVER. *On Black Film: A Film and Lecture Series Presented by the Annenberg Center for the Communication Arts and Sciences, University of Pennsylvania.* Philadelphia, 1973. A useful compendium of interview, filmography, and articles.

GLAESSNER, VERINA. *Kung Fu: Cinema of Vengeance.* New York:

Bounty Books, 1974. A good anatomy of the genre that usurped young black audience attention in the declining years of "blaxploitation" movies.

————. "The Negro in Contemporary Cinema." *Film* (Spring 1971): n.p.

GOLDWYN, RONALD. *"The Scar of Shame." Discover* [*Sunday Bulletin* (Philadelphia)], November 17, 1974: 14–23. The best article on the provenance of one black film.

GREEN, THEOPHILUS. "The Black Man as Movie Hero." *Ebony* XXVII (August 1972): 144–48.

GULLIVER, ADELAID CROMWELL, ed. *Black Images in Films: Stereotyping and Self-Perception as Viewed by Black Actresses.* Boston: Boston University Afro-American Studies Program, 1974. A symposium with Susan Batson, Cynthia Belgrave, Ruby Dee, Beah Richards, and Cicely Tyson, with essays by Joseph Boskin, Carlton Moss, and Thomas Cripps.

HARRIS, MIDDLETON, comp. *The Black Book.* New York: Random House, 1974. Good for its few illustrations of ephemera such as black movie posters.

HENNEBELLE, GUY. *L'Afrique Literaire et Artistique: Les Cinemas Africains en 1972.* Dakar, Senegal: Société Africaine d'Edition, 1972. A source of otherwise inaccessible data.

HIGGINS, CHESTER. "Black Films: Boom or Bust." *Jet* XLII (June 8, 1972): n.p.

HIPPENMEYER, JEAN-ROLAND. *Jazz sur Films ou 55 Années de Rapports Jazz-Cinema vus a travers plus de 800 Films tournés entre 1917 et 1972.* Yverdon, Switzerland: Editions de la Thiele, 1973. The most thorough of several European chronicles of jazz-film.

HOBERMAN, JIM. "A Forgotten Black Cinema Surfaces." *Village Voice* (New York), November 17, 1975, 1 ff. See also *New York Daily News,* March 9, 1975.

HUGHES, LANGSTON, and MILTON MELTZER, eds. *Black Magic: A Pictorial History of the Negro in American Entertainment.* Englewood Cliffs, N. J.: Prentice-Hall, 1967. A survey with a brief section on film, illustrated with stills.

HURD, LAURA E. "Director Ossie Davis Talks About *Black Girl." Black Creation* IV (Winter 1973): 38–39. A rare interview with a practicing black director.

"Jam Session in Movieland." *Ebony* I (November 1945): 6–9. A postwar black liberal estimate of *Jammin' the Blues.*

JEROME, V. J. *The Negro in Hollywood Films.* New York: Masses & Mainstream, 1950.

JOHNSON, ALBERT. "Beige, Brown or Black." *Film Quarterly* XIII (Fall 1959): 38–43.

————. "The Negro in American Films: Some Recent Works." *Film Quarterly* XVIII (Summer 1965): 14–30.

KAGAN, NORMAN. "Black American Cinema." *Cinema* VI (Fall 1970): 2–7. A derivative piece.

KAMINSKY, STUART M. *American Film Genres: Approaches to a Critical Theory of Popular Film.* New York: Laurel Edition, 1977.

KOTLOWITZ, ROBERT. "The Making of *Angel Levine.*" In *Film 69/70,* edited by Joseph Morgenstern and Stefan Kanfer, pp. 175–81. New York: Simon and Schuster, 1970. A rare essay on the problems of production.

LANDAY, EILEEN. *Black Film Stars.* New York: Drake, 1973. A hardback fan letter.

LEAB, DANIEL J. "The Black in Films: An Annotated Bibliography." *Journal of Popular Film* IV (1975), 345–56.

————. *From Sambo to Superspade: The Black Experience in Motion Pictures.* Boston: Houghton Mifflin, 1975.

LIMBACHER, JAMES L. "Blacks on Film: A Selected List . . . ." *Journal of Popular Film* IV (1975): 358–78.

————, and BARBARA BRYANT. *Minorities in Film I. Minorities in Film II. Minorities in Film III.* In "Shadows on the Wall" TV series. Detroit: Wayne State University College of Lifelong Learning, 1975.

MAPP, EDWARD. *Blacks in American Films: Today and Yesterday.* Metuchen, N. J.: Scarecrow Press, 1972.

MATTOX, MICHAEL. "The Day Black Movie Stars Got Militant." *Black Creation* IV (Winter 1973): 40–42. A breezy account of the founding and work of the Black Artists Alliance.

MAYNARD, RICHARD A. *The Black Man on Film: Racial Stereotyping.* Rochelle Park, N.J.: Hayden Book, 1974. A small book that rescues a few important pieces from oblivion, among them Floyd Covington's "The Negro Invades Hollywood," an optimistic article on black employment in Hollywood in the 1920s from the Urban League organ, *Opportunity;* Robert Benchley's review of *Hallelujah!* and Sterling Brown's assault on *Imitation of Life,* both for *Opportunity;* Ralph Ellison's careful essay on *Intruder in the Dust;* James Baldwin's barbed review of *Carmen Jones;* and several pointed comments on recent black movies from *New York Times* critics.

METZ, CHRISTIAN. *Film Language: A Semiotics of the Cinema.* New York: Oxford University Press, 1974. An important work for understanding genre film in terms of structural linguistics.

MICHENER, CHARLES. "Black Movies." *Newsweek* LXXV (October 23, 1972): 74–82. In *Black Man on Film,* edited by Richard A. Maynard, pp. 96–104. One of several critical pieces on the rise of the blaxploitation film.

"Mister Washington Goes to Town." Time XXXV (April 29, 1940): 84. An unusual review of a black film in a white magazine.

MOSS, CARLTON. "The Negro in American Films." *Freedomways* III (Spring 1963): 134–42.

MUNDEN, KENNETH J. "A Contribution to the Psychological Understanding of the Cowboy and His Myth." *American Imago* XV (Summer 1958): 103–48. A pioneer work on film seen as myth.

————, ed. *The American Film Institute Catalog of Motion Pictures Produced in the United States, 1921–1930.* New York: R. R. Bowker, 1971. One of a series in progress that will catalog all American films. A useful topical index allows a close examination of black film production, although no indication is made as to whether a film survives or where it is located.

MURRAY, JAMES P. "A Futuristic Fable." *Black Creation* IV (Winter 1973): 43. Fanciful anatomy of elements necessary to accomplish a black film tradition.

————. "The Subject is Money." *Black Creation* IV (Winter 1973): 26 ff. Details on the obstacles facing prospective black filmmakers in Hollywood.

————. *To Find an Image: Black Films from Uncle Tom to Super Fly.* Indianapolis: Bobbs-Merrill, 1973.

NOBLE, PETER, *The Negro in Films.* London: S. Robinson, 1948.

PATTERSON, LINDSAY. *Black Films and Film-makers: A Comprehensive Anthology from Stereotype of Superhero.* New York: Dodd, Mead, 1975. The best available anthology. It includes familiar pieces such as Richard Wesley's "Which Way the Black Film," from *Encore*; Maurice Peterson's *"Book of Numbers"*, an account of the making of a film, from *Essence*; and Pauline Kael's long, careful *New Yorker* story, "Notes on Black Movies."

PEAVY, CHARLES D. "Black Consciousness and the Contemporary Cinema." In *Popular Culture and the Expanding Consciousness,* edited by Ray B. Browne. New York: Wiley, 1973. The best essay on the impact of modern cinema on blacks.

PINES, JIM. *Blacks in the Cinema: The Changing Image.* London: Studio Vista, 1971. A polemical pamphlet published on the occasion of a British Film Institute black film series, and later expanded into the present book. A curiously interesting, though flawed, expatriate perspective.

POUSSAINT, ALVIN. "Cheap Thrills That Degrade Blacks." *Psychology Today* VII (February 1974): 22, 26–27, 30, 38, 98. An essay by another hostile witness in the trial of blaxploitation movies.

PROPP, VLADIMIR. *The Morphology of the Folk Tale.* Austin, Tex.: University of Texas Press, 1968. Structuralism applied to folklore, a useful tool for students of American film genres.

RILEY, CLAYTON. "What Makes Sweetback Run?" *New York Times,* May 9, 1971, sec. 2, p. 4.

SAMPSON, HENRY T. *Blacks in Black and White: A Source Book on Black Films.* Metuchen, N. J.: Scarecrow Press, 1977. A pioneering effort to make a research tool.

SHALES, TOM. *"The Emperor Jones."* In *The American Film Heritage: Impressions from the American Film Institute Archives,* edited by Tom Shales, Kevin Brownlow, *et al.,* pp. 70–74. Washington, D. C.: Acropolis Books, 1972. A brief recent critical essay.

SOLOMON, STANLEY J. *Beyond Formula: American Film Genres.* New York: Harcourt Brace Jovanovich, 1976.

"Spirit of Youth." Time XXXI (January 31, 1938): 35–37. A review of Grand National's biography of Joe Louis.

TATE, CECIL F. *The Search for a Method in American Studies.* Minneapolis: University of Minnesota Press, 1973. A useful sampling of possible methods of interpreting genre film, based on the work of Henry Nash Smith, Roy Harvey Pearce, John Ward, and R. W. B. Lewis.

THOMPSON, ROBERT FARRIS. "An Aesthetic of the Cool." *African Arts* VII (Autumn 1973): 41–43, 64–67, 89–92. An important and earnest attempt to sketch a prologomena to understanding *aesthetique du cool.*

TUDOR, ANDREW. *Image and Influence: Studies in the Sociology of Film.* London: Allen & Unwin, 1974. A sensible book, willing to take risks in the cause of seeking a social basis for understanding movies. A good criticism of structuralists and semiologists with a good chapter on genres.

VAN PEEBLES, MELVIN. *Sweet Sweetback's Baadasssss Song.* New York: Lancer Books, 1971. A self-consciously outrageous and scatological history of the making of the title movie. The best single expression of the outlawry and rebellion that black intellectual genre filmmakers hoped would become the identifying mode of the genre.

VIDOR, KING. *A Tree is a Tree.* New York: Harcourt, Brace, 1953. Vidor's autobiography, with a chapter on *Hallelujah!*

WARD, RENEE. "Black Films, White Profits." *Black Scholar* VII (May 1976): 13–25.

WARNER, VIRGINIA. *"The Negro Soldier:* A Challenge to Hollywood." In *The Documentary Tradition from Nanook to Woodstock,* edited by Lewis Jacobs, pp. 224–25. New York: Hopkinson and Blake, 1971.

WARSHOW, ROBERT. *The Immediate Experience.* Garden City, N. Y.: Doubleday, 1964. Contains two essays on genre that have elicited almost worshipful praise for their sensitive insights.

WRIGHT, WILL. *Six Guns and Society: A Structural Study of the Western.* Berkeley: University of California Press, 1975. The first attempt to study a popular film genre using the methods of the structural anthropologists.

ZITO, STEPHEN. "The Black Film Experience." In *The American Film Heritage: Impressions from the American Film Institute Archives,* edited by Tom Shales, Kevin Brownlow, *et al.,* pp. 61–69. Washington, D. C.: Acropolis Books, 1972. A good early statement of the aspirations of race movies.

In addition to these essays, the regional black press as well as the *New York Times,* often carries both light and serious comment on black film. Reviews of specific films may be found also by checking the *Times* index and comparing it with other newspapers and magazines. Also the *Readers' Guide to Periodical Literature* provides a handy source for the discovery of otherwise fugitive pieces, along with research centers that promise to develop from programs of Chamba Productions in New York, the Oakland Museum in California, and the recently opened black archive of the Academy of Motion Picture Arts and Sciences in Beverly Hills.

Appendix A   The Credits

The Scar of Shame
Produced by Colored Players Film Corporation
Released 1927
Direction   Frank Perugini
Story   David Starkman
Cinematographer   Al Ligouri

Cast
ALVIN HILLIARD   Harry Henderson
LOUISE   Lucia Lynn Moses
LOUISE'S FATHER   William E. Pettus
THE LANDLADY   Ann Kennedy
EDDIE   Norman Johnstone
MISS HATHAWAY   Pearl McCormick
MR. HATHAWAY   Lawrence Chenault

Rental Source: Standard Film Service, 14710 West Warren Avenue, Dearborn, Michigan 48126.

The St. Louis Blues
Presented by Radio Pictures
Distributed by RKO Distributing Corporation
Copyright 1929
Story and Direction   Dudley Murphy
Editor   Russell G. Shields
Cinematographer   Walter Strenge
Recordist   George Oschmann
Choral Arrangements   W. C. Handy and J. Rosamond Johnson

Cast
BESSIE   Bessie Smith
THE ST. LOUIS WOMAN   Isabel Washington
JIMMY   Jimmy Mordecai
JANITOR   Alex [*sic*] Lovejoy
[LITTLE MAN]   [Edgar Connor]

Jimmy Johnson's Orchestra
The W. C. Handy and J. Rosamond Johnson Choir

Rental Sources: Kit Parker Films, Carmel, California; Standard Film Service, 14710 West Warren Avenue, Dearborn, Michigan 48126.

Blood of Jesus
Distributed by Sack Amusement Enterprises
Produced by Amegro Films
Copyright 1941
Direction   Spencer Williams
Screenplay   Spencer Williams
Cinematography   Jack Whitman
Sound Recording   R. E. Byers

Cast
SISTER JACKSON   Cathryn Caviness
RAS JACKSON   Spencer Williams
SISTER JENKINS   Juanita Riley
SISTER ELLERBY   Reather Hardeman
THE ANGEL   Rogenia Goldthwaite
SATAN   Jas. B. Jones [*sic*]
JUDAS GREEN   Frank H. McClennan
RUFUS BROWN   Eddie De Base
LUKE WILLOWS   Alva Fuller
   and
Rev. R. L. Robertson and The Heavenly Choir

Rental Source: Film Classic Exchange, 1926 South Vermont Avenue, Los Angeles, California 90007.

The Negro Soldier
Presented by The War Department
Produced by Special Coverage Section, United States Army Signal Corps
Released 1943
Premiere   London, August, 1943

Supervisor   Colonel Frank Capra
Director   Captain Stuart Heisler
Writer and narrator   Carlton Moss
Music   Dimitri Tiomkin
Mr. Tiomkin's Staff   William Grant Still, Earl Robinson, Al Glasser,
                 Howard Jackson, Phil Moore, Calvin Jackson,
                 Jester Hairston, Corporal Dave Tamkin
First Cameraman   Lieutenant Paul C. Vogel
Second Cameramen   Captain Horace Woodard, Chief Petty Officer
                 Alan Thompson
Assistant Cameramen   Sergeants William Birch, Jack Hageny, Lloyd
                 Fromm
Chief Electrician   Sergeant Howard Roberts
Production Grips   Sergeants Cecil Axemear, Ed Comport
First Assistant Directors   Lieutenants Lee Katz and Holly Morse, and
                 George Blair and Ralph Donaldson
Second Assistant Director   Corporal Mort Lewis
Technical Advisor   Carlton Moss
Film Cutter   Sergeant Jack Ogilvie
Assistant Film Cutter   Sergeant Hugh Fowler
Sound Cutter   Corporal Tom Macdoo
Music Cutter   Jimmy Graham
Assistant Music Cutter   Sergeant Ed Hare
Chief of Sound   Lieutenant William Montague
Sound Crew   Sergeant Harold Lee, Corporal William Hamilton, Private
                 Cyril Harper
Church Set Design   Haldane Douglas
Special Effects   Consolidated Laboratories, Ray Mercer, Albert
                 Schmidt, Gordon Jennings, Farciot Edouart, Paul
                 Lerpae
Production Manager   Captain Ralph Nelson
Consultant   Major Charles Dollard
Liaison Officer   Captain Maurice Monette
"Grateful acknowledgement is made to Mr. Joe Swerling for his
aid in preparing the script."

Cast
CHIEF CHARACTERS   Men and Women of the Armed Forces of the
    United States
THE HEROES   Private Robert Brooks, Captain Colin Kelly, Sergeant
    Meyer Levin, Dorie Miller

CHURCH SOLOIST   Sergeant Clyde Turner
MINISTER   Carlton Moss
JIM   William Broadus
MRS. BRONSON   Bertha Wolford
ROBERT BRONSON   Lieutenant Norman Ford
CHAPLAIN   Clarence Brooks

"Choir under the direction of Jester Hairston and Army Air Force
Orchestra, Major Eddie Dunstedter, Conductor"

Rental Source: University of Colorado, Bureau of Audio Visual
Instruction, Stadium Building, Boulder, Colorado 80302.

Nothing But a Man
Produced by Nothing But a Man Company, Inc.
Presented by Roemer-Young and DuArt
Premiere New York, November 27, 1964

Producers   Robert Young, Michael Roemer, and Robert Rubin, in
associaton with DuArt Film Laboratories
Screenplay   Michael Roemer and Robert Young
Direction   Michael Roemer
Editor   Luke Bennett
Cinematography   Robert Young
Sound   Robert Rubin
Unit Manager   William Rhodes
Assistant Cameraman   Peter Vollstadt
Electrician   Frank Sukosd (by arrangement with Bay State Film
Productions, Inc.)
Location Manager   Philip Clarkson
Assistant   Clayton Riley
Costumer   Nancy Ruffing
Secretary   Sandi Nelson
Associate Editor   Robert Machover
Assistant Editor   Peter Gessner
Services   Cal Penny
Sound Mixer   Albert Gramaglia
Harmonica   Wilbur Kirk
Titles   F. Hillsberg, Inc.
Musical Performances   Mary Wells, The Gospel Stars, Martha and
the Vandellas, The Miracles, Holland Dozier,
Little Stevie Wonder, The Marvelettes (by
arrangement with Motown Record Corporation)

Cast
DUFF   Ivan Dixon
JOSIE   Abbey Lincoln
LEE   Gloria Foster
WILL   Julius Harris
MILL WORKER   Martin Priest
FRANKIE   Leonard Parker
JOCKO   Yaphet Kotto
REVEREND DAWSON   Stanley Greene
EFFIE   Helen Lounck
DORIS   Helene Arrindell
CAR OWNER   Walter Wilson
POP   Milton Williams
RIDDICK   Melvin Stewart
REVIVALIST   Reverend Marshall Tompkins
BARNEY   Alfred Puryear
JOE   Charles McRae
WILLIE   Ed Rowan
TEENAGERS   Tom Ligon and William Jordan
SOLOIST   Dorothy Hall
MRS. DAWSON   Gertrude Jeanette
MILL FOREMAN   Gil Rogers
GARAGE OWNER   Richard Webber
SUPERINTENDENT   Eugene Woods
BAR MAN   Jim Wright
HIRING BOSS   Arland Schubert
STOREKEEPER   Peter Carew
GIN FOREMAN   Bill Riola
UNDERTAKER   Jay Brooks
DESK CLERK   Robert Berger
BESSIE   Jary Banks
MILL HANDS   Richard Ward and Moses Gunn
CAR PASSENGERS   Mark Shapiro and William Phillips
CHURCH WOMEN   Sylvia Ray, Esther Rolle, and Evelyn Davis

Rental Sources: Association Instructional Materials, 866 Third Avenue,
New York, New York 10022; University of California, Extension Media
Center, 2223 Fulton Street, Berkeley, California 94720; Impact Films,
144 Bleecker Street, New York, New York 10012; Macmillan Films,
34 McQuesten Parkway South, Mount Vernon, New York 10550.

Sweet Sweetback's Baadasssss Song
Produced by Yeah, Inc.
Presented by Melvin Van Peebles and Jerry Gross
Released by Cinemation Industries
Premiere March, 1971 in Detroit and April, 1971 in Atlanta
"This film is dedicated to all the Brothers and Sisters who had enough of the Man."
"Sire, these lines are not a homage to brutality that the artist has invented, but a hymn from the mouth of reality."—traditional prologue of the dark ages ["supered" in French and English]
Story and Direction   "A Film of Melvin Van Peebles"
Director of Photography   Bob Maxwell
Cinematographers   Bob Maxwell and Jose Garcia
Production Manager and Assistant Director   Clyde Houston
Makeup Supervisor   Nora Maxwell
Assistant Editor   Jeremy Hoenack
Sound   Clark Wall
Special Effects   Cliff Wenger
Second Unit Director   Jose Garcia
Optical Effects   Muller-Curtis-O'Neill and CFI
Sound Editors   John Newman and Luke Wolfram
Dubbing   Art Piantadosi
Orchestra and Orchestrations   Earth, Wind and Fire
Titles and Processing   CFI
"Come on Feet"   A & M Records
Sweetback's Wardrobe   Mr. B's S Fashions of LA

Cast
"Starring the Black Community and Br'er Soul"
Co-starring

Simon Chuckster	Nick Ferrari
Hubert Scales	Ed Rue
John Dullaghan	Johnny Amos
West Gale	Lavelle Roby
Niva Rochelle	Ted Hayden
Rhetta Hughes	[and Melvin Van Peebles]

With

Mario Peebles	Jeff Goodman
Sonja Dunson	Curt Matson
Michael Agustus	Marria Evonee

Peter Russell
Norman Fields
Ron Prince
Steve Cole
Megan Peebles
Joe Tornatore
Mike Angel
The Copeland Family

Jon Jacobs
Bill Kirschner
Vincent Barbi
Chet Norris
Joni Watkins
Jerry Days
John Allen
Bruce Adams

Rental Sources: Warner Brothers, Non-Theatrical Division, 4000 Warner Boulevard, Burbank, California 91503.

Appendix B Filmography of Black Genre Films

Filmography

A Natural Born Gambler (USA, 1916)   Bert Williams [?]

Body and Soul (USA, 1924)   Oscar Micheaux

Ten Nights in a Bar Room (USA, 1926)   Colored Players [Frank Perugini?]

Eleven P. M. (USA, 1928)   Richard D. Maurice

Melancholy Dame (USA, 1928)   Spencer Williams [?]

Voyage au Congo (France, 1928)   Marc Allegret

Black and Tan (USA, 1929)   Dudley Murphy

Borderline (Switzerland, 1929)   Kenneth Macpherson

Hallelujah! (USA, 1929)   King Vidor [and Harold Garrison?]

Hearts in Dixie (USA, 1929)   Paul Sloane [and Clarence Muse?]

The Exile (USA, 1931)   Oscar Micheaux

The Black King (USA, 1932)   Donald Heywood

Drums o' Voodoo (USA, 1933)   Arthur Hoerle [and J. Augustus Smith?]

The Emperor Jones (USA, 1933)   Dudley Murphy

Sanders of the River (Britain, 1935)   Zoltan Korda

Symphony in Black (USA, 1935)   Fred Waller

Dark Manhattan (USA, 1937)   George Randol

Jericho (Britain, 1937)   Thornton Freeland

One Mile from Heaven (USA, 1937)   Alan Dwan

Song of Freedom (Britain, 1937)   J. Elder Wills

Spirit of Youth (USA, 1937)   Harry Fraser

Keep Punching (USA, 1939)   John Clein

Moon over Harlem (USA, 1939)   Edgar G. Ulmer

Paradise in Harlem (USA, 1939)   Joseph Seiden

Way Down South (USA, 1939)   Bernard Vorhaus

Broken Strings (USA, 1940)   Bernard B. Ray
One Tenth of Our Nation (USA, 1940)   Henwar Rodakiewiecz
Proud Valley (Britain, 1940)   Pen Tennyson
Murder on Lennox [sic] Avenue (USA, 1941)   Arthur Dreifuss
Henry Brown, Farmer (USA, 1942)   Roger Barlow
Boogie Woogie Dream (USA, 1944)   Bert and Jack Goldberg
Go Down Death (USA, 1944)   Spencer Williams
Stormy Weather (USA, 1943)   Andrew Stone
Reet, Petite, and Gone (USA, 1947)   Bud Pollard
Man of Two Worlds (Britain, 1947)   Thorold Dickinson
The Quiet One (USA, 1948)   Sidney Meyers
Jim Comes to Jo'burg (South Africa, 1949)   Donald Swanson
Native Son (Argentina, 1951)   Pierre Chenal
Bright Road (USA, 1953)   Gerald Mayer
Anna Lucasta (USA, 1958)   Philip Yordan
Jazz on a Summer's Day (USA, 1959)   Bert Stern
The Cry of Jazz (USA, 1959)   Edward Bland
Come Back Africa (USA, 1959)   Lionel Rogosin
Porgy and Bess (USA, 1959)   Otto Preminger
Take a Giant Step (USA, 1959)   Philip Leacock
A Raisin in the Sun (USA, 1961)   Daniel Petrie
Sunday on the River (USA, 1961)   Gordon Hitchens and Ken Resnick
Gone are the Days (USA, 1963)   Nicholas Webster
Lilies of the Field (USA, 1963)   Ralph Nelson
The Cool World (USA, 1963)   Shirley Clarke
Dutchman (USA, Britain, 1967)   Anthony Harvey
Sweet Love Bitter (USA, 1967)   Herbert Danska
For Love of Ivy (USA, 1968)   Daniel Mann
Up Tight (USA, 1968)   Jules Dassin
Still a Brother (USA, 1968)   William Greaves and William Branch
The Learning Tree (USA, 1968)   Gordon Parks
No Vietnamese Ever Called Me Nigger (USA, 1968)   David Loeb
    Weiss
Putney Swope (USA, 1969)   Robert Downey
Onkel Tom's Hutte (Yugoslav-German, 1969)   Gerza Radvanyi
The Great White Hope (USA, 1969)   Martin Ritt
Slaves (USA, 1969)   Herbert J. Biberman
Watermelon Man (USA, 1970)   Melvin Van Peebles
Cotton Comes to Harlem (USA, 1970)   Ossie Davis
Eldridge Cleaver (France, 1970)   William Klein

Kongi's Harvest (Nigeria, 1970)   Ossie Davis
Martin Luther King: A Filmed Record. . . . (USA, 1970)   Ely Landau
Shaft (USA, 1970)   Gordon Parks
The Murder of Fred Hampton (USA, 1971)   Mike Grey
Right On! (USA, 1971)   Herbert Danska
Soul to Soul (USA, 1971)   Denis Sanders
The Bus is Coming (USA, 1971)   Wendell Franklin
Melinda (USA, 1971)   Hugh Robertson
Black Girl (USA, 1972)   Ossie Davis
Blood's Way (USA, 1972)   Stan Taylor
The Book of Numbers (USA, 1972)   Raymond St. Jacques
Come Back Charleston Blue (USA, 1972)   Mark Warren
Malcolm X (USA, 1972)   Arnold Perl and Martin Worth
Five on the Black Hand Side (USA, 1973)   Oscar Williams
Ganja and Hess (USA, 1973)   Bill Gunn
The Harder They Come (Jamaica, 1973)   Perry Henzel
Harlem: Voices, Faces (Sweden, 1973)   Lars Ulvenstam and Tomas
     Dillen
Let the Church Say Amen (USA, 1973)   St. Claire Bourne
Save the Children (USA, 1973)   Stan Lathan
The Spook Who Sat by the Door (USA, 1973)   Ivan Dixon [and Sam
     Greenlee]
Wattstax (USA, 1973)   Mel Stuart
Willie Dynamite (USA, 1973)   Gilbert Moses
The Autobiography of Miss Jane Pittman (USA, 1974)   John Korty
American Shoeshine (USA, 1975)   Sparky Greene
From These Roots (USA, 1975)   William Greaves
Harvest: Year 2000 (Ethiopia, 1975)   Haile Gerima
Countdown at Kusini (USA, 1975)   Ossie Davis
Black Shadows on a Silver Screen (USA, 1975)   Steven York
Smile Orange (Jamaica, 1975)   Trevor Rhone
Tuskegee Subject #626 (USA, 1975)   Leroy McDonald
Coonskin (USA, 1976)   Ralph Bakshi
The Long Night (USA, 1976)   Woodie King
Passing Through (USA, 1977)   Larry Clarke

Index